Al Gore

Other books in the People in the News series:

Al Gore

by Laurie Collier Hillstrom

LUCENT BOOKS
A part of Gale, Cengage Learning

GALE
CENGAGE Learning™

Detroit • New York • San Francisco • New Haven, Conn • Waterville, Maine • London

LIBRARY OF CONGRESS CATALOGING-IN-PUBLICATION DATA

Hillstrom, Laurie Collier, 1965-
  Al Gore / by Laurie Collier Hillstrom.
    p. cm. — (People in the news)
  Includes bibliographical references and index.
  ISBN 978-1-4205-0086-8 (hardcover)
  1. Gore, Albert, 1948—Juvenile literature. 2. Vice-Presidents—United States—
Biography—Juvenile literature. I. Title.
  E840.8.G65H565 2009
  973.929092—dc22
  [B]
                                                        2008033857

Lucent Books
27500 Drake Rd
Farmington Hills MI 48331

ISBN-13: 978-1-4205-0086-8
ISBN-10: 1-4205-0086-4

Printed in the United States of America
1 2 3 4 5 6 7 12 11 10 09 08

Contents

Fame and celebrity are alluring. People are drawn to those who walk in fame's spotlight, whether they are known for great accomplishments or for notorious deeds. The lives of the famous pique public interest and attract attention, perhaps because their experiences seem in some ways so different from, yet in other ways so similar to, our own.

Newspapers, magazines, and television regularly capitalize on this fascination with celebrity by running profiles of famous people. For example, television programs such as *Entertainment Tonight* devote all their programming to stories about entertainment and entertainers. Magazines such as *People* fill their pages with stories of the private lives of famous people. Even newspapers, newsmagazines, and television news frequently delve into the lives of well-known personalities. Despite the number of articles and programs, few provide more than a superficial glimpse at their subjects.

Lucent's People in the News series offers young readers a deeper look into the lives of today's newsmakers, the influences that have shaped them, and the impact they have had in their fields of endeavor and on other people's lives. The subjects of the series hail from many disciplines and walks of life. They include authors, musicians, athletes, political leaders, entertainers, entrepreneurs, and others who have made a mark on modern life and who, in many cases, will continue to do so for years to come.

These biographies are more than factual chronicles. Each book emphasizes the contributions, accomplishments, or deeds that have brought fame or notoriety to the individual and shows how that person has influenced modern life. Authors portray their subjects in a realistic, unsentimental light. For example, Bill Gates—the cofounder and chief executive officer of the software giant Microsoft—has been instrumental in making personal computers the most vital tool of the modern age. Few dispute his business savvy, his perseverance, or his technical expertise, yet critics say he is ruthless in his dealings with competitors and driven more by his desire to maintain Microsoft's dominance in the computer industry than by an interest in furthering technology.

In these books, young readers will encounter inspiring stories about real people who achieved success despite enormous obstacles. Oprah Winfrey—the most powerful, most watched, and wealthiest woman on television today—spent the first six years of her life in the care of her grandparents while her unwed mother sought work and a better life elsewhere. Her adolescence was colored by promiscuity, pregnancy at age fourteen, rape, and sexual abuse.

Each author documents and supports his or her work with an array of primary and secondary source quotations taken from diaries, letters, speeches, and interviews. All quotes are footnoted to show readers exactly how and where biographers derive their information and provide guidance for further research. The quotations enliven the text by giving readers eyewitness views of the life and accomplishments of each person covered in the People in the News series.

In addition, each book in the series includes photographs, annotated bibliographies, timelines, and comprehensive indexes. For both the casual reader and the student researcher, the People in the News series offers insight into the lives of today's newsmakers—people who shape the way we live, work, and play in the modern age.

A Life in the Spotlight

From the day he was born in 1948, Al Gore appeared to be destined for great things. As the son of a powerful U.S. senator, he was groomed for a life in public service from an early age. Gore's parents gave him a top-notch education at an exclusive prep school in Washington, D.C. They introduced him to important political figures and helped him understand the inner workings of government. They also taught him the value of hard work and humility during summers on the family farm in Tennessee.

After graduating from Harvard University with a bachelor's degree in government, Gore enlisted in the U.S. Army and served in the Vietnam War. Aside from feeling a sense of patriotic duty, Gore had other reasons for choosing military service. He hoped that it would aid both his father's Senate reelection campaign and his own later chances for a political career.

Gore launched that career in 1976, at the age of twenty-eight, when he ran successfully for a seat in the U.S. House of Representatives. Eight years later he followed in his father's footsteps and was elected to represent Tennessee in the U.S. Senate. In 1988—before he even reached the age of forty—the high-achieving Gore ran for president. Although he failed to win the Democratic Party nomination, Gore gained national name recognition.

The unsuccessful 1988 campaign put Gore in a good position to become Bill Clinton's vice presidential running mate in 1992.

Al Gore's legacy of public service and environmental activism has earned him admiration and respect both in the United States and around the world.

Once elected, the two youthful southern moderates forged a true partnership that made Gore one of the most active and influential vice presidents in American history. Clinton and Gore worked closely together throughout the administration's two terms in office.

As the 2000 election approached, many observers believed that Gore was ideally positioned to become the next president of the United States. He coasted to the Democratic nomination and in many ways appeared better qualified to lead the country than his Republican opponent, George W. Bush.

As the weeks passed, though, Gore's presidential campaign veered off track. Many of the advantages Gore had spent a life-time cultivating seemed to turn into disadvantages. His broad experience in politics led critics to describe him as a privileged Washington insider who did not understand the concerns of ordi-nary Americans. His loyal service in the Clinton administration became a negative in the minds of voters who claimed that the president had failed to demonstrate integrity and moral values in the White House. Gore also experienced image problems in the media and had trouble connecting with voters.

The 2000 election turned out to be one of the closest in U.S. history. Due to a dispute over vote totals in Florida, the winner could not be determined for nearly five weeks. Finally, the U.S. Supreme Court stepped in to halt the recounting of ballots in Florida and declare Bush the winner of the election.

The controversial Supreme Court decision dealt Gore a crushing blow. It ended his career in politics, shook his faith in American democracy, and forced him to reassess his life and his future plans. But the terrible disappointment also helped Gore change in positive ways and gave him the opportunity to forge a new path of public service.

When Gore returned to the spotlight, he appeared newly confident and at ease with himself. Liberated from politics, he committed tremendous energy and passion to raising public awareness of the threat of global warming. The Academy Award-winning documentary film *An Inconvenient Truth* delivered Gore's alarming message about the potential consequences of climate change to millions of people around the world. In 2007 he received the Nobel Peace Prize for his work toward solving the climate crisis. Gore's fearless crusade helped him become one of the most visible and effective environmental activists in the world. To many observers, the respect and admiration he earned for these efforts made it seem that Gore fulfilled his destiny after all.

Chapter 1

Two Separate Childhoods

Al Gore grew up in two different worlds. During the school year, he lived on the top floor of a fancy hotel in Washington, D.C. Over the summers, he worked on his family's farm in rural Tennessee. Both of these environments helped shape Gore's development as a person. "Just as having two eyes gives you depth perception, having two homes allows you to see some things that stand out in relief when viewed from two different perspectives,"[1] he stated.

Born into a Political Family

Albert Alfred Gore Jr.—known as Al—was born on March 31, 1948, in Washington, D.C. His father, Albert Gore Sr., was a member of the U.S. Congress. A Democrat, he had first been elected to serve his home state of Tennessee in the U.S. House of Representatives in 1939. Al's mother, Pauline LaFon Gore, was one of the first women to graduate from law school at Vanderbilt University in Tennessee. Instead of working as a lawyer, though, she became an active political wife. She organized her husband's election campaigns, hosted and attended many social events, and did volunteer work for the Democratic Party.

Albert and Pauline Gore were thrilled when Al was born. They already had a daughter, Nancy, who had been born in 1938. But they had also wanted a son, and they had almost given up hope when baby Al finally arrived. His excited parents called the

Four-year-old Al, lower right, stands with his family outside of their apartment in Nashville, Tennessee, in 1952. From left are his sister, Nancy, and his parents, Pauline and Senator Albert Gore Sr.

editors of the *Nashville Tennessean*—the biggest newspaper in their home state—and insisted that they publish his birth announcement on the front page.

A Child in an Adult World

When Al was four years old, his father ran for a seat in the one-hundred-member U.S. Senate. Albert Gore won the election and took office in 1953. At this point, the Gore family moved into a

Nine-year-old Al gives his mother, Pauline, a goodnight kiss outside of his family's apartment at the Fairfax Hotel before she and Al's father, Senator Albert Gore Sr., head to a formal White House event in 1957.

Albert Gore, Sr.

Al Gore has often described his father as one of the most important influences in his life. Albert Gore Sr. was born in 1907. He grew up poor on a small farm in Possum Hollow, Tennessee. He went to a one-room schoolhouse as a boy and later worked his way through college and law school. Gore was a teacher and school superintendent before he entered politics in 1938.

After serving in the U.S. House of Representatives for fourteen years, Gore won a seat in the U.S. Senate in 1952. At this time, Tennessee and most other southern states practiced segregation, or the forced separation of people by race. They had laws that required black people and white people to use separate public facilities, including schools, restrooms, and drinking fountains. Two years after Gore joined the Senate, the U.S. Supreme Court declared segregation laws illegal and ordered the southern states to integrate schools and other public facilities. Many white people in the South disagreed with the Court ruling, and they expected their elected representatives to argue against integration.

Senator Gore, however, supported the Court ruling and promoted civil rights for African Americans. Some white southerners called him a traitor, but many others—including his young son—admired him for standing up for his beliefs. "Growing up, I watched him stand courageously for civil rights, economic opportunity, and a government that worked for ordinary people," Al Gore stated.

During the 1960s, Albert Gore became known for his opposition to the Vietnam War. This position was unpopular in the South, and some critics called him un-American. His antiwar position contributed to his losing his seat in the Senate in 1971. After he left politics, Albert Gore served on the boards of several corporations and opened a law firm. He actively supported his son's political career until his death in 1998, at the age of ninety.

Al Gore, "Facing the Crisis of Spirit," *Vital Speeches of the Day*, August 15, 1992, p. 647.

Albert Gore Sr. served his home state of Tennessee in both the House and Senate for over thirty years.

two-bedroom apartment on the eighth floor of the Fairfax Hotel in Washington, D.C. Their apartment overlooked Rock Creek Park and the embassies of several foreign countries.

Young Al's early years in Washington were marked by loneliness. Most of his neighbors were involved in politics and held powerful positions in the federal government, but they had few young children. Other than a few school friends, Al did not have many playmates his own age. "There were not a lot of kids around the Fairfax," recalled his childhood friend Steve Armistead. "The friend he had in the Fairfax was a bellhop. There were all these dignitaries, but not much for a kid. There was a dullness, a loneliness about it."[2]

The busy schedules that his parents maintained also contributed to Al's loneliness. Albert and Pauline Gore often traveled on Senate business or made campaign visits to Tennessee. When his parents went out of town, Al usually stayed at the Fairfax in the care of a nanny or a babysitter.

An Early Exposure to Politics

Being the son of a senator, however, also gave Al some unique opportunities. Senator Gore hoped that Al would follow in his footsteps one day and make a career in politics. In fact, Al's parents often told their friends that they wanted him to become president someday. During Al's boyhood, they tried to prepare him for a life in public service by exposing him to important people and teaching him about the political process.

As part of this preparation, Albert Gore sometimes took his son with him to the Senate office building. If the senator was not too busy, they played catch in the hallway outside his office. Al also attended a number of Senate hearings throughout his youth. He listened as members of Congress held long, detailed discussions about various issues and legislation.

When Al was fourteen years old, his father received an unexpected telephone call from President John F. Kennedy. Senator Gore had been working with representatives from several labor unions on a deal that would help stabilize the price of American steel. The president called him at home to complain about steel industry executives, who seemed determined to undermine the deal. Without knowing what the call was about, Albert Gore allowed his son to listen in on an extension. Al ended up hearing the president express his anger and frustration in very colorful language. "Al came back into the dining room," his father remembered, and said, "Whew, Daddy, I didn't know presidents talked like that!"[3]

Albert and Pauline Gore also exposed their children to politics through conversations at the dinner table. The senator often asked his family's opinion about the different bills before Congress. They also talked about current events and issues, such

The Gore family strolls near the Capitol Building in 1957. Life in Washington, D.C., as the son of a senator, allowed young Al to witness government in action and meet many prominent political figures.

as the civil rights movement. By the time he reached his teens, Al had formed his own opinions about some political issues. But he generally tended to be polite, respectful, and agreeable during these family discussions. His older sister, on the other hand, was independent-minded and rebellious. She often challenged their parents' ideas, as well as their authority. Still, Nancy Gore proved to be an important source of advice and support for Al, especially when their parents were not available.

An Elite Education

Another way in which Al's parents prepared him for public service was by providing him with a top-notch education. Starting in fourth grade, Al attended an exclusive, private preparatory school called the St. Albans Episcopal School for Boys. The campus was located on the grounds of the National Cathedral, just a few blocks from the Fairfax Hotel. Many high-ranking government officials sent their sons to St. Albans. The school set high stan-

The Dignity of Public Service

Throughout Al Gore's career in politics, critics often described his speaking style as stiff, wooden, and formal. He claimed that he inherited this tendency from his father. As a politician, Albert Gore felt it was important to show respect for his office by presenting himself in a dignified manner. "Some of what people perceive as the stiffness and formality I sometimes lapse into comes in part from my father's habit of trying to ensure that he always presented a dignified appearance to live up to the position he felt deserved dignity," Gore explained. "He had a capacity to enjoy humor and music and friendship, and he also felt the need to present himself as a senator in a formal and dignified way."

Melinda Henneberger, "Al Gore's Journey: A Boyhood Divided," *New York Times on the Web*, May 22, 2000. http://partners.nytimes.com/library/politics/camp/052200wh-dem-gore.html?scp=1&sq=Al%20GOre's%20Journey:%20A%20BOy's%20LIfe%20in%20and%20OUt%20of%20the%20Family%20Script&st=cse.

dards of academic achievement, good manners, and citizenship for its students. All of the boys who attended were required to wear a uniform that included a jacket and tie.

Fellow students at St. Albans remember Al as being serious, competitive, and a little bit stuffy during his school years. Although he scored very high on intelligence tests, Al's grades usually ranked in the middle of his class. His favorite subject was art. He loved to paint and showed some early artistic talent.

In 1961 Al entered high school at St. Albans. He played on the basketball team and proved to be an accurate outside shooter. He also threw the discus as a member of the track team. During his senior year, Al served as captain of the football team. Unfortunately, the team lost seven games that year and only earned one victory. In addition to playing sports, Al also served as class treasurer and belonged to the government club and the glee club.

Al also occasionally attended dances sponsored by the school. Shortly before graduating from high school in 1965, Al went to a dance in which St. Albans hosted students from St. Agnes, a local girls' prep school. At this event, Al met a smart, lively, attractive young woman who would eventually become his wife. Her full name was Mary Elizabeth Aitcheson, but she had been known by the nickname "Tipper" since childhood. Tipper loved music and played the drums in an all-girl band. Although she had attended the dance with one of Al's friends, Al liked her so much that he called her the next day to ask for a date. She ended up coming to visit him on the family farm in Tennessee that summer.

A Tennessee Farm Boy

Throughout his years as a student at St. Albans, Al returned to Tennessee every summer and on most holidays. His family owned a 500-acre farm near the small town of Carthage, about 60 miles east of Nashville. His parents felt it was important for the family to maintain a connection to the place and people that Senator Gore represented in Congress.

Although Al had been born in Washington, D.C., he considered Tennessee his true home. He always preferred to spend his time at the farm instead of at the Fairfax. "If you're a boy, and you have the choice between the eighth floor of a hotel and a big farm with horses, cows, canoes, and a river, it was an easy choice for me,"[4] he declared.

Throughout his childhood, Al identified with the people of Carthage and formed many close relationships there. He also felt deep emotional ties to his life on the farm. "He didn't lay around Washington much when he could have been in Carthage," said his childhood friend Steve Armistead, "and that's where he got his values, working on the farm and growing up around Smith County people."[5]

During his time in Tennessee, Al enjoyed all the benefits of being a country boy. He went canoeing on the Cumberland and Caney Fork rivers, for instance, and went swimming and boating on nearby lakes. He showed Angus cattle in the county fair and won several blue ribbons over the years. Al also had fun hanging around with a large group of friends. "We did all the experimental things kids do," Steve Armistead recalled. "We'd sneak out at night and pick up Coke bottles off a front porch that probably were not ours, or go to the lake and maybe do a little waterskiing at night that was not too smart, and occasionally have a party."[6]

The Gore farm had a lot to offer a boy, but the time Al spent there was not all fun and games. His father expected him to work hard during the summer. He got up early every morning to feed the chickens, horses, cows, and pigs. His daily chores also included cleaning the barns and shoveling manure. Al spent most afternoons working in the fields alongside the farmhands his father hired. They cleared land, baled hay, and cut tobacco. Albert Gore made his son perform so much hard, physical labor that the hired help sometimes felt sorry for the boy. But Al understood that his father wanted to teach him the value of hard work. "He must have told me a hundred times the importance of learning how to work,"[7] he remembered.

When Al Gore grew up and followed in his father's footsteps, his political opponents often described him as the privileged son of a senator. They accused him of overstating his Tennessee roots in an effort to seem more folksy and down-to-earth to voters. But Al, as well as his friends and family, insisted that he formed a genuine connection to the land and people of Tennessee during his youth. His experiences on the family farm—as much as his experiences in the nation's capital—helped shape his outlook on life.

Chapter 2

From Harvard to Vietnam

The years 1965 to 1975 were ones of education and personal growth for Al Gore. He attended Harvard University, got married, served in the U.S. Army during the Vietnam War, and worked as a newspaper reporter. Although Gore remained unsure of his future plans during this period, all of these experiences helped him grow more mature and independent.

Becomes a Harvard Man

After graduating from St. Albans School in 1965, Gore was accepted at Harvard University, a prestigious school located in the leafy Boston suburb of Cambridge, Massachusetts. Once he arrived on campus, Gore immediately established himself as an active member of Harvard's class of 1969. He spent his second day on campus knocking on the doors of dormitory rooms, introducing himself to fellow students, and asking them to vote for him in a successful campaign to become president of the freshman class. In addition to participating in student government, Gore made the Harvard basketball team as a freshman. He saw limited playing time, however, and averaged only three points per game.

Between his classes, extracurricular activities, and dorm life, Gore developed a large circle of friends. One of his best friends at Harvard was Tommy Lee Jones, who went on to become an Academy Award-winning actor. He also became good friends with

Gore, shown here in his college yearbook photo, was active both academically and socially during his years at Harvard University.

one of his English professors, Erich Segal, who later published the best-selling novel *Love Story*. Segal used Gore, Jones, and other Harvard students as inspiration for the main character in the book.

Gore's college friends knew him as a serious, reserved, and competitive young man who sometimes showed a lighter, fun-loving side. He enjoyed hanging out in the dorm and listening to music, watching episodes of *Star Trek* on television, and playing poker late into the night. Once in a while, Gore challenged his friends to some sort of goofy contest. The friendly competitions he organized ranged from throwing knives at trees to swimming across the Charles River.

Beginning in his sophomore year, Gore also spent a lot of time with his girlfriend, Tipper Aitcheson. A year younger than Gore, she joined him in Boston in 1966, after she graduated from high school. While Gore attended Harvard, Tipper studied child psychology at nearby Garland Junior College and Boston University. They got together as much as possible to hang out in his dorm room, take long walks around campus, and go out on dates.

College Professors Influence His Views

Gore did not let his active social life distract him from his academic studies during his time at Harvard. He felt fortunate to be exposed to interesting issues and new ideas by professors who were leaders in their fields, such as political scholar Richard Neustadt. Gore credits Neustadt with inspiring him to pursue a major in government.

During his senior year, Gore took another course that had a significant impact on him. To fulfill a science requirement, he signed up for a class taught by the respected oceanographer and geophysicist Roger Revelle. Revelle was one of the first scientists to conduct a long-term study of the amount of carbon dioxide in the Earth's atmosphere. With the help of several international scientific organizations, he took atmospheric samples from around the world over a period of eight years.

Revelle's research showed that the concentration of carbon dioxide in the atmosphere was increasing rapidly. The professor attributed the increase to two main factors: a worldwide increase in the burning of fossil fuels, which produced carbon dioxide; and

The Vietnam War

During Al Gore's college years, the United States was deeply affected by its involvement in the Vietnam War. The Southeast Asian nation of Vietnam had been divided into two parts in 1954, as part of a peace agreement that ended French colonial rule in the region. North Vietnam was controlled by Communist forces, and South Vietnam was led by a U.S.-backed government.

The leaders of North Vietnam wanted to reunite the two halves of the country under Communist rule. Their plan received support from powerful Communist nations like China and the Soviet Union. It also held appeal for some residents of South Vietnam, who formed a guerilla army known as the Viet Cong to provide secret aid to the Communists.

U.S. leaders were determined to prevent South Vietnam from falling into Communist hands. At that time, the United States and the Soviet Union were involved in a period of intense military and political rivalry known as the Cold War. Both sides were trying to increase their power and influence around the world. Many Americans worried that a Communist takeover of South Vietnam would threaten U.S. security. The government provided increasing amounts of military and economic aid to help South Vietnam fight off the Communists.

In 1965 the first American ground troops were sent into combat against the North Vietnamese army and their Viet Cong allies. American military involvement escalated quickly, until the number of U.S. troops in Vietnam reached 500,000 in 1969. Despite this huge commitment, though, the U.S. and South Vietnamese forces had little success against their determined enemies. The war turned into a bloody stalemate that killed or wounded thousands of American soldiers and huge numbers of Vietnamese.

Many Americans were upset that U.S. leaders chose to intervene in the Vietnam War. Critics questioned both the reasons for going to war and the way in which the fighting was conducted. Large-scale antiwar protests took place throughout the late 1960s and early 1970s. Some of the most violent demonstrations took place on American college campuses.

U.S. troops withdrew from Vietnam in 1973, shortly after the two sides signed a peace agreement. North Vietnam continued its efforts to take over South Vietnam, however, and succeeded in reuniting the country under Communist rule in 1975.

a worldwide decrease in the amount of land covered by forests, which turned carbon dioxide into oxygen. Revelle suggested that the rising levels of carbon dioxide from these trends could trap heat in the atmosphere—creating what he called a greenhouse effect—and result in higher average temperatures on Earth.

To Gore, Revelle's early work on global warming was a revelation. "It felt like such a privilege to be able to hear about the readouts from some of those measurements in a group of no more than a dozen undergraduates. Here was this teacher presenting something not years old but fresh out of the lab, with profound implications for our future!"[8] he recalled. "It taught me that nature is not immune to our presence, and that we could actually change the makeup of the entire earth's atmosphere in a fundamental way."[9] Revelle's course raised Gore's interest in environmental issues and had a profound influence on his later career.

Turmoil in the Outside World

Gore graduated from Harvard in June 1969 with a bachelor's degree in government. Throughout his college years, American society was going through a period of great turmoil and change. The 1960s marked the peak of the civil rights movement, when African Americans fought to end racial discrimination and gain equal rights and opportunities. It also saw the growth of the women's liberation movement, which encouraged American women to break out of their traditional roles as wives and mothers and fight for greater freedom and equality.

Another controversial issue affecting the nation during Gore's college years was the Vietnam War. Many Americans disagreed with the U.S. government's decision to send military forces to Vietnam. They also disliked the draft system that the government used to select men for military service. As the war dragged on and grew more unpopular, antiwar protests took place across the country. College students were especially vocal in their opposition to U.S. military involvement in Vietnam.

A number of antiwar protests took place at Harvard during Gore's years as a student. Gore personally opposed U.S. military

Young people across the nation, like these students at the University of California at Berkeley, actively turned out at marches and rallies in the late 1960s and early 1970s to protest the Vietnam War.

involvement in Vietnam, but he did not play an active role in the antiwar movement at Harvard. He often felt that the student demonstrators hurt their cause by being too confrontational. Still, Vietnam played a major role in Gore's college experience. He and his friends spent hours debating about the war, the draft, anti-war protests, civil rights marches, race riots, and the country's future. Concerns about these issues weighed heavily on the minds of Gore, his fellow students, and millions of other Americans. "Throughout our four years at Harvard, the nation's spirits sank,[10] he recalled.

Decides to Join the Army

As the date of Gore's graduation from Harvard approached, he faced important decisions about his future. As soon as he left college, Gore would lose his student deferment and become eligible for the military draft. He did not support the war, and he knew that he could probably find a legal way to avoid going

The Draft

Once Al Gore graduated from college, he became eligible for the military draft. The draft is a method that the U.S. government sometimes uses to fill the ranks of the armed forces when not enough people volunteer to serve. A government agency called the Selective Service collects the names of all American men between the ages of eighteen and twenty-six. During the Vietnam War, draft offices across the country drew names randomly. When his name was drawn, a man was required to report to his local draft board for evaluation.

A man who was drafted either had to report for duty in the armed forces, or had to qualify for a deferment (an official delay of military service). The Selective Service typically granted deferments to men who had physical problems, were needed at home to support a family, worked in an industry that was vital to the war effort, or were enrolled in college full time. Some men also avoided serving in Vietnam by joining the National Guard, which allowed them to fulfill their military obligation in the United States.

The military draft contributed to many people's negative view of the Vietnam War. The government's use of the draft meant that many soldiers served in Vietnam against their will. Critics questioned whether these soldiers had the commitment and discipline needed to perform effectively in a war zone.

In addition, many people felt that the draft system unfairly discriminated against the poor, minorities, and recent immigrants. They pointed out that wealthy, educated, white Americans were much better equipped to take advantage of the legal methods for delaying or avoiding military service. As a result, the majority of draftees in Vietnam came from poor or working-class families from the nation's urban centers and rural areas.

Demonstrators burn a draft card and induction notice to protest the military draft, which forced many young men to serve in the Vietnam War against their will.

to Vietnam. A friend of the family had saved him a spot in the Tennessee National Guard, for example. Taking this position would allow him to fulfill his military obligation with little risk of being sent overseas. Gore also considered keeping his student deferment by enrolling in graduate school.

At the same time, though, a number of factors pulled Gore toward military service. For one thing, he worried that avoiding the draft might hurt his father's political career. Albert Gore Sr. was one of the leading antiwar voices in the U.S. Senate, and he faced a tough reelection campaign in 1970. President Richard Nixon and his Republican allies made it a priority to defeat Gore and other antiwar Democrats in Congress. Al Gore feared that if he avoided military service, he would give ammunition to his father's political enemies. He also recognized that serving in Vietnam could help his own chances of making a career in politics someday.

Another factor driving Gore toward military service was his sense of fairness. He knew that many other young men who had registered for the draft in rural Tennessee did not have any options to avoid military service. "I realized that if I decided not to go and figured out some way to get out of it, that would mean somebody else from my hometown would go instead of me," Gore noted. "I thought about that a lot. I felt that would outweigh my own personal calculation of the rights and wrongs about the country's policy."[11]

Gore agonized over the decision throughout his senior year of college. After weighing his options and discussing the matter with friends and family, he finally decided to join the U.S. Army. Rather than waiting to be drafted, Gore enlisted in the service on August 7, 1969. Gore's choice set him apart from most of his fellow students at Harvard. Of the 1,100 men in his graduating class, only about a dozen ended up serving in the military. All of the other Harvard graduates who joined the military entered as officers, which placed them in command of lower-ranking soldiers and gave them more influence over their duty assignments. In contrast, Gore chose to enter as a private—the lowest rank in the army—since that was the main option available to other young men from rural Tennessee.

Serves in the United States Army

Shortly after enlisting, Gore completed his basic military training at Fort Dix in New Jersey. He was then assigned to work as a military journalist at Fort Rucker in Alabama. Fort Rucker was an important training school for helicopter pilots and crews who flew missions in Vietnam.

On his way to the army base, Gore stopped in Cambridge to say good-bye to some of his friends and professors. He was surprised at the strong reaction he got from Harvard students as he walked across campus in his army uniform. A number of students jeered at him or made obscene gestures. "It was an amazing experience," he recalled. "I was the same person inside but my physical appearance conveyed a message that completely overwhelmed the message of my humanity. It was just an emotional field of negativity and disapproval and piercing glances that shot arrows of what certainly felt like real hatred, and I was astonished."[12]

Gore spent the next year stationed at Fort Rucker. During this time, he married his longtime girlfriend, Tipper Aitcheson. The couple exchanged vows on May 19, 1970, at the National Cathedral in Washington, D.C. Gore wore his military dress uniform for the ceremony. After the wedding, Tipper came to live with him in a trailer near the army base.

Senator Albert Gore Sr. and his wife Pauline, right, greet Al and his bride, Tipper, on their wedding day in May 1970.

During breaks from his work on the army newspaper at Fort Rucker, Gore returned to Tennessee to campaign for his father. At the time, Albert Gore was locked in a tight Senate race against Republican challenger Bill Brock, who was strongly supported by the Nixon administration. Al Gore appeared in several campaign TV commercials and made public appearances around the state on behalf of his father. Gore always wore his army uniform in campaign appearances. The idea was to show that even though his father opposed the Vietnam War, the senator was still a good, patriotic American.

In the meantime, Gore anxiously awaited orders to ship off to Vietnam. He eventually began to suspect that the Nixon administration intentionally held up his combat orders. Gore reasoned that the president could not take a chance on the son of a prominent antiwar senator being killed or wounded in battle, because then his father might receive enough sympathy votes to boost him to reelection. Gore was never able to prove his suspicions, and several administration officials denied it. Still, the situation bothered him. "All I know is, I was not allowed to go until the first departure date after the November election,"[13] he noted.

Despite his son's assistance, Albert Gore Sr. lost his bid for reelection in November 1970. It was a difficult time for the Gore family, and it caused Al Jr. to become disillusioned with the American political system. Before long, though, a new worry occupied his parents' minds. Shortly after his father lost his seat in the Senate, Gore finally received his orders to go to Vietnam.

Ships off to Vietnam

Gore left the United States after Christmas 1970 and arrived in Vietnam on January 2, 1971. He was assigned as an army journalist to cover the activities of the Twentieth Engineer Brigade in Bien Hoa. Even before he arrived, the other soldiers in his unit knew that he had political connections. A general instructed the men to keep an eye on him and try to prevent him from getting hurt. "The general said that it was not an order, but that he requested that we keep a very close eye on this individual and

Gore, standing second from right, gathers with other soldiers serving in Vietnam in 1971. While performing his duties as an army journalist, Gore refused any special treatment and earned the respect of his comrades.

that we try to keep him out of harm's way," remembered army photographer Alan Leo. "I actually had some negative feelings toward him before I even met him, for the simple reason that he was getting special treatment."[14]

Once Gore arrived in Vietnam, however, he made every effort to become one of the guys. He insisted that he be treated just like everyone else, and he soon earned the respect of his fellow soldiers. Like most army journalists, Gore spent much of his time in areas that were relatively secure. He never came under enemy fire or had to shoot anyone. "I've never claimed to have been in combat," he acknowledged. "No way would I compare what I did with people who came through the fire and did brave things."[15] By most accounts, though, Gore took more risks than he needed to take in Vietnam. For instance, he often flew into combat areas by helicopter shortly after battles concluded to interview the participants.

For the final month of his tour in Vietnam, Gore joined the Army Engineer Command in Long Binh, near Saigon. He reported on the activities of army engineers who paved roads, built bridges, and did other work to support the war effort. Gore sent some of his articles to friends and family members back in the United States. A few of these articles were published in his hometown paper, the *Nashville Tennessean*. The editors there were impressed by his research and writing skills.

Gore received an honorable discharge from the army two months before his official term of service ended. He later observed that his Vietnam experience:

> Didn't change my conclusions about the war being a terrible mistake, but it struck me that opponents to the war, including myself, really did not take into account the fact that there were an awful lot of south Vietnamese who desperately wanted to hang on to what they called freedom. Coming face to face with those sentiments expressed by people who did the laundry and ran the restaurants and worked in the fields was something I was naively unprepared for.[16]

Works as a Newspaper Reporter

When Gore returned to the United States in the summer of 1971, he enrolled in divinity school at Vanderbilt University in Nashville. "I wanted a structured opportunity to explore the deeper questions in my life,"[17] Gore explained. During this same period, Gore contacted John Siegenthaler, an editor at the *Nashville Tennessean* and a longtime supporter of his father. Impressed by Gore's work as a military journalist, Siegenthaler offered him a job as a reporter. Once Gore completed his year at Vanderbilt, he went to work for the paper full time.

As a rookie reporter, Gore started out writing about parades, festivals, and other local events. He enjoyed his work as a reporter, but he

As a rookie reporter for the **Nashville Tennessean,** *Gore,* *shown here consulting with a photographer, covered local events and avoided political stories.*

was not sure whether he wanted to make a lifelong career in journalism. Gore explored several other possibilities during the early 1970s. For instance, he became a partner in a land development company and oversaw the construction of a subdivision. Gore also tried his hand at farming. He bought some land in Carthage, just across the river from his childhood home, and used it to raise livestock and grow tobacco. Gore also became a father when Tipper gave birth to a daughter, Karenna, on August 6, 1973.

Gore also continued working as a journalist. As he moved on to more important assignments covering crime and politics, he developed a reputation as a smart and aggressive reporter. Gore found his experience as an investigative journalist very exciting. But he also grew frustrated at his inability to make positive changes to the city government. These feelings convinced Gore to go to law school. He hoped that a legal education would give him a greater opportunity to address problems that he saw in American government and society. He took a leave of absence from the paper and began taking law classes at Vanderbilt.

Chapter 3

Following in His Father's Footsteps

After resisting the idea for many years, Al Gore finally decided to follow in his father's footsteps and launch a career in politics. In 1976 he campaigned successfully for a seat in the U.S. House of Representatives. After serving four terms in the House, he was elected to represent Tennessee in the U.S. Senate in 1984.

Throughout his time in Congress, Gore earned a reputation as a hard-working, detail-oriented public servant who had a strong understanding of highly technical issues. However, a failed bid for the Democratic presidential nomination in 1988—followed by a near-fatal accident involving his young son in 1989—led Gore to rethink his priorities.

Jumps into Politics

In the mid-1970s Gore still had no intention of entering politics. Memories of the painful end of his father's long career in public service made him reluctant to consider the idea. In February 1976, however, Tennessee congressman Joe Evins announced his retirement from the U.S. House of Representatives. Evins occupied the same seat that Gore's father had held before he joined the Senate. He also represented the district that included Carthage, where the younger Gore had bought a farm. Since this particular seat might not open up again for a generation, Gore decided to quit law school and run for Congress. "It just came home to me that if I was ever going to do it, now was the time," he remembered. "Not ten years from now. Not one week from now. Now."[18]

Gore announced his candidacy on the steps of the county courthouse in Carthage. He told the gathered crowd of friends, family members, and other supporters that he did not plan to rely on his father's legacy during his campaign. "I don't want the people to vote for or against me because my name is Albert Gore," he stated. "I want to speak on the issues, and the people of the Fourth District are perfectly capable of judging me on this basis."[19]

Gore's main opponent in the Democratic primary was Stanley Rogers, a member of the Tennessee state legislature. Rogers argued that Gore was too young and inexperienced to represent the state in the federal government. He also claimed that Gore had grown up as a child of privilege in Washington, and therefore was out of touch with the people of rural Tennessee.

Gore overcame these charges by running a spirited campaign. He traveled extensively within his district, visiting town halls, roadside diners, and farms. "He just embraced these people," recalled David Lyons, who covered the campaign for the *Nashville Banner*. "He didn't embrace them physically, but he was genuinely interested in what people had to say. . . . He didn't sound like everybody thought he would sound—like Prince Albert."[20]

Gore also won over voters by presenting himself as a political moderate who would be tough on crime and oppose new gun-control laws. His positions on these issues reflected the values of voters in his district. Thanks to his effective campaign strategies, Gore defeated Rogers in the Democratic primary. He then cruised to an easy victory in the general election.

Becomes a Forward-Thinking Member of the House

When Gore took office in January 1977, he and his family moved to the Washington suburb of Arlington, Virginia. They settled into the modest house where Tipper had spent her childhood. A few months later, Tipper gave birth to a second daughter, Kristin.

Tipper Gore Campaigns for Warning Labels on Explicit Music

While Al Gore served in Congress, his wife Tipper stayed busy as well. In addition to being a wife and mother, she also earned a master's degree in psychology and became involved in a number of volunteer activities. Tipper Gore is probably best known for her campaign to place warning labels on record albums that contained explicit lyrics.

Tipper first grew concerned about the content of popular music in the early 1980s. The Gores' eldest daughter, Karenna, was a big fan of Prince and bought his album *Purple Rain*. Tipper was appalled by the sexually suggestive lyrics it contained. She found many other examples of obscene language, violence, and sexual imagery in songs by other artists who were popular among teenagers. She decided that parents needed to know about the explicit content of music in order to protect their children.

In 1984 Tipper launched an organization called the Parents' Music Resource Center (PMRC). The group asked the Recording Industry Association of America (RIAA) to develop a rating system—like that used in the movie industry—to inform parents about explicit lyrics. In 1985 Tipper testified before Congress in favor of warning labels for records. She also published a book on the topic, called *Raising PG Kids in an X-Rated Society*.

Tipper's campaign received a great deal of support from parents' groups and the general public. But it also generated a storm of criticism from the entertainment industry. Many recording artists complained that Tipper wanted to censor their creative expression or ban rock music entirely. Some political analysts warned that Tipper's high-profile campaign might hurt her husband's career.

The PMRC and the RIAA eventually reached an agreement to put a label on controversial material that read Explicit Lyrics—Parental Advisory. Al Gore expressed support for his wife's activities. "I am very proud of what she has done," he

continued

Tipper Gore testifies before the Senate in September 1985 as part of her campaign for warning labels on records containing explicit lyrics.

stated. "I think we as a society ought to ask questions about how we raise children in this culture and pay more attention to elevating the awareness of us all about the messages that young children get."

Bob Zelnick, *Gore: A Political Life*. Washington, DC: Regnery, 1999, p. 142.

Gore holds two cans of baby food that were part of a recall in 1979, prompting his work as a member of the House to establish nutritional and safety standards for the product.

Although his new job and growing family kept him busy, Gore returned to Tennessee often. He remembered that political opponents had accused his father of becoming a Washington insider and losing touch with the people he represented. Gore was determined to avoid that kind of criticism in his own political career. "He went back to Tennessee three weeks out of four," said longtime aide Roy Neel. "He held literally thousands of open meetings, town meetings, across the state."[21]

Keeping in touch with voters helped Gore get elected to a second term in 1978. The following year, his daughter Sarah was born. Gore's experiences as a father had an influence on his work as a legislator. For instance, he helped pass a bill that required the use of flame-resistant materials in children's pajamas. He also sponsored a bill that established nutritional and safety standards for baby formula. These victories helped him win a third term in 1980.

Another issue that interested Gore during his service in the House was technology. He loved to study scientific advances, often immersing himself in the smallest details of cutting-edge research. Some of the high-tech issues Gore tackled as a legislator included alternative energy sources, nuclear weapon systems, and organ transplants. He also took a strong interest in new communication methods, such as a new cable television network dedicated to showing Congress in action. On March 19, 1979, Gore became the first legislator to appear on the new network, C-SPAN.

Wins a Seat in the U.S. Senate

Gore was reelected for a fourth term in Congress in 1982. He also welcomed the birth of his son, Albert III, that year. Two years later, Howard Baker, a Republican who had represented Tennessee in the U.S. Senate for many years, announced his decision to retire. Gore immediately announced his intention to run for Baker's seat in the Senate.

During his election campaign, Gore ran as a moderate. He described himself to Tennessee voters as "someone who wants to make certain that the Democratic Party continues its move to the center, into the mainstream of American thought."[22] This campaign strategy, along with his voting record as a member of the House, helped him win the election by a wide margin.

Vice President George Bush, right, administers the oath of office to newly elected Senator Al Gore in January 1985 while Gore's wife, Tipper, second from right, and their daughters look on.

After joining the Senate, Gore continued to focus on many of the issues that had interested him earlier in his political career. As a member of the Senate Armed Services Committee, for instance, he worked on bills relating to weapons systems and arms control agreements. His interest in science and technology also led to a position on the Commerce, Science, and Transportation Committee, where he played an important role in securing government funding for development of the Internet.

As Gore's service in the Senate continued, though, he also moved toward more liberal positions on several social issues, including abortion. He supported pro-choice positions much more frequently than he had as a member of the House. Gore's record on tobacco legislation also showed evidence of a shift in his views. In the House, Gore represented a Tennessee district that was full of tobacco farmers. As a result, he often voted in favor of government policies that supported tobacco growers and increased tobacco prices. During Gore's 1984 Senate campaign, however, his sister Nancy died of lung cancer. Knowing that smoking had contributed to his sister's death, Gore pushed for stronger health warnings on cigarette packages during his years in the Senate. "Until I draw my last breath, I will pour my heart and soul into the cause of protecting our children from the dangers of smoking,"[23] he declared. Some critics felt that Gore was being inconsistent by supporting tobacco growers but opposing the use of their products.

Runs for President

Gore enjoyed the challenge of dealing with difficult issues as a member of the Senate. As a lawmaker, though, he felt limited in his ability to influence government policy and direct the country's future. He sometimes found it hard to convince his fellow senators to take action on issues that he felt held national importance, such

Gore gives a speech as part of his run for the Democratic presidential nomination in February 1988. His campaign platform focused on environmental issues, which did not spark the interest of the voters or the press.

Al Gore's Role in Building the Internet

Throughout his service in the U.S. Congress, Al Gore was known for his forward-thinking approach to high-tech issues. He made some of his most important contributions in this area by promoting the development of the Internet. Long before most of his colleagues had even heard of computer networks, Gore made speeches about the potential benefits of a national "information superhighway." He spoke with leading computer researchers, learned about the problems they faced in linking the nation's major computer systems together, and introduced a bill to help them address those problems. This legislation, the High Performance Computing and Communication Act of 1991, helped create the vast public computer network that became the Internet.

Years later, Gore discussed his legislative work in an interview for CNN. "During my service in the United States Congress," he told Wolf Blitzer, "I took the initiative in creating the Internet." This comment led to harsh criticism from Gore's political opponents. A Republican Party press release made the false claim that Gore had tried to take credit for "inventing" the Internet. The national news media repeated this claim and used it as evidence that Gore was prone to wild exaggerations. The story contributed to negative public perceptions of Gore as someone who was willing to mislead voters or even lie about his record in order to get elected.

Many Internet historians, however, feel that the criticism Gore received was unfair. He was an early champion of computer networking technology during his years in Congress. And the statement he made is considered to be a fairly accurate description of his contribution. The real inventors of the Internet—computer researchers Vinton Cerf and Bob Kahn—have confirmed the importance of Gore's legislative work in making the modern Internet possible. "We don't think, as some people have argued, that Gore intended to claim he 'invented' the Internet," they declared. "Moreover, there is no question in our minds that while serving as Senator, Gore's as environmental protection and global warming. For these reasons, Gore started to think about running for president someday.

After carefully weighing his chances, Gore decided to enter the 1988 presidential race. His father, who had once dreamed of becoming president himself, was thrilled to hear the news. "I had ambitions for the presidency—it didn't turn out that way," the elder Gore noted. "I've been negotiating with the Lord to let me live to see that something like that happens [to my son]."[24]

After announcing his candidacy, Gore initially tried to make environmental issues the main focus of his campaign. "One of the main reasons I ran was to try to elevate the importance of the [environmental] crisis as a political issue,"[25] he explained. Gore spoke about the threat of global warming and the impact of increasing human population on the world's limited resources. As the campaign continued, however, polls showed that many Americans were not interested in hearing about the environment. Gore then shifted his strategy and presented himself as a moderate who could work with members of both political parties to accomplish national goals. "I simply lacked the strength to keep on talking about the environmental crisis constantly whether it was being reported in the press or not,"[26] he later admitted.

Gore focused his campaign on the South. He hoped that a strong showing in the Super Tuesday primaries could give his candidacy momentum in other parts of the country. Unfortunately for Gore, his strategy did not work. Gore did receive the most votes in five southern states, including his home state of Tennessee, but Massachusetts governor Michael Dukakis won the two biggest states, Texas and

Florida. After Dukakis went on to win the New York primary, Gore reluctantly bowed out of the race. Dukakis clinched the party nomination a few weeks later, but he lost to Republican candidate George H.W. Bush in the November 1988 election.

Rethinks His Priorities

Gore went back to work in the Senate, but a few months later his life took a frightening turn. On April 3, 1989, Gore and his wife took their six-year-old son, Albert, to see the Baltimore Orioles play on Major League Baseball's opening day. As they left the stadium afterward, Albert broke away from his parents and ran into a busy street. He was hit by a car. "Tipper and I watched as he was thrown 30 feet through the air, and scraped another 20 feet on the pavement after he hit the ground,"[27] Gore recalled.

Young Albert suffered severe injuries, including broken ribs, a broken leg, a broken collarbone, and damage to his internal organs. He also had a concussion and was in a coma for several days. Albert spent three weeks in the hospital and underwent surgery several times. Even when he was finally able to go home, he had to wear a full-body cast for three months.

Gore spent countless hours at his son's bedside throughout his long recovery. During this time, he decided that spending time with his family was more important than advancing his political career. He decided against running for president again in 1992. "I would like to be president, but I am also a father, and I feel deeply about my responsibility to my children,"[28] he stated.

Instead of campaigning, Gore planned to focus his political energy squarely on the issue that he felt most strongly about: protecting the environment. "When you've seen your six-year-old son fighting for his life, you realize that some things matter a lot more than winning," he explained. "You realize that we were not put here on earth to look out for our needs alone."[29]

As part of his work to protect the environment, Gore wrote a book called *Earth in the Balance* that outlined his views. Gore claimed that the planet had suffered terrible damage from careless and wasteful human activities. He argued that people needed to

Gore carries his son Albert out of the hospital three weeks after the six-year-old boy was struck by a car and severely injured in April 1989. Gore's experience helping Albert through his lengthy recovery led to his decision not to attempt a presidential run in 1992.

change their habits and actively conserve resources. "Each of us must take a greater personal responsibility for this deteriorating global environment," he wrote. "Each of us must take a hard look at the habits of mind and action that reflect—and have led to—this grave crisis."[30] Gore also issued a warning about global climate change and the negative impact it could have on Earth.

Despite its intense subject matter and scientific emphasis, Gore's book turned out to be one of the publishing sensations of 1992. *Earth in the Balance* became a best-seller, and it lifted its author to a new level of national prominence.

Chapter 4

The Clinton-Gore Years

After serving sixteen years in Congress, Al Gore went on to serve eight years as vice president of the United States under President Bill Clinton. As bright, ambitious, youthful, moderate Democrats from the South, Gore and Clinton had a great deal in common. They forged a partnership that enabled Gore to become one of the most active and influential vice presidents in American history.

Watches the 1992 Presidential Race

Even though Gore had decided not to run for president in 1992, he watched the campaign with great interest. On the Republican side, President George H.W. Bush was running for reelection. During the first half of 1991, it looked like the president would easily defeat any of the possible Democratic candidates to win a second term in office. Bush was very popular at that time because he led the United States to an impressive victory in the Persian Gulf War.

As the year wore on, however, many voters shifted their attention away from the successful war effort and toward the faltering U.S. economy. Business failures and unemployment rates had increased, and many people believed that Bush did not understand the economic anxiety felt by ordinary Americans. In addition, conservatives were outraged when Bush approved a tax

Democratic presidential nominee Bill Clinton, right, clasps hands with running mate Gore as they wave to the crowd at the 1992 Democratic National Convention.

increase in violation of a 1988 campaign pledge. Bush suddenly appeared vulnerable in the 1992 election.

A number of prominent Democrats took notice of Bush's downturn in popularity and decided to run for president. Bill Clinton, who was serving his fifth term as the governor of Arkansas, announced his candidacy in October 1991. Clinton was genuinely passionate about government policymaking, and he had a smooth and charming manner that helped him connect with ordinary people. He also had an appealing message. Clinton's campaign focused on voters' concerns about the economy. He promised to work with Republican leaders to downsize the federal government, balance the national budget, and provide greater access to health care for all Americans.

Clinton's campaign faltered in the early going, stung by criticisms of his lack of foreign policy experience and accusations of immoral personal behavior. But the candidate recovered, and in the spring of 1992 Clinton was the Democratic presidential nominee. Clinton then set about choosing a vice presidential running mate. Most presidential candidates try to choose a running mate who can best help them win the election by appealing to a different set of voters. For this reason, most tickets tend to feature running mates from different age groups and geographical regions.

With these factors in mind, the Clinton campaign considered a number of potential running mates, including Gore. Clinton advisors were aware that many voters already knew Gore from his 1988 presidential campaign and his best-selling book *Earth in the Balance*. In addition, Gore's strengths seemed to balance out some of Clinton's perceived weaknesses. Unlike Clinton, Gore had a strong foreign policy background and had served in Vietnam.

Gore was flattered to be considered, but he was not sure whether he was interested in the job. He had decided not to run for president in 1992 because he wanted to spend more time with his family. He worried that campaigning for and serving as vice president would prove nearly as time consuming and disruptive to his family life.

Another factor in Gore's decision was the nature of the job. The role of the vice president is not well-defined in the U.S. Constitution. The vice president is first in line for the presidency if the president is unable to complete his term in office. The vice president also casts the deciding vote in case of a tie in the Senate. Other than that, though, the vice president's responsibilities are left to the judgment of the president. In many previous administrations, the vice presidency had been mostly a symbolic or ceremonial position. Gore was only interested in the job if he had important tasks to perform and a real influence on the president's policy decisions.

Despite his concerns, Gore agreed to meet with Clinton in June 1992 to discuss the vice presidency. The two men barely knew each other before this time, but they immediately connected both personally and politically. In fact, what was supposed to be an hour-long interview ended up stretching late into the night. "He and Clinton met like college pals who had not seen each other since the 1960s and were picking up where they had left off," David Maraniss and Ellen Nakashima wrote in *The Prince of Tennessee.* "They could show each other how smart they were and how much they knew without provoking the normal feelings of jealousy or tension. They were not competing directly, they were sensing what it would be like if they combined to take on the rest of the world."[31]

As they talked, Gore's intelligence, discipline, and sense of loyalty impressed Clinton. He assured Gore that his vice president would be a true partner and play an important role in the administration. Gore became convinced that serving as Clinton's vice president would give him the opportunity to make positive changes to the country. A few days later, Clinton called to offer Gore the job. After talking it over with his family, Gore accepted.

On the Campaign Trail

Clinton officially received the Democratic presidential nomination at the party's national convention in early July. Although he had already announced his selection of Gore as his running mate,

Gore addresses voters while Bill Clinton looks on during one of the many stops the candidates made on their cross-country campaign bus tour leading up to the 1992 election.

Gore officially received the vice presidential nomination on July 9, 1992. At the convention, Clinton promised that Gore would "assume a strong role in the Clinton administration, a role of genuine leadership in the areas of his passion and expertise."[32]

Gore began proving his value to the ticket shortly after he received the nomination. He gave an emotional acceptance speech at the convention that surprised people who had expected him to deliver a dull policy-oriented address. Gore talked about his son's injury and how the long, difficult recovery process had affected him and his family. He then expressed his determination to bring a similar type of healing to the nation. "My friends, if you look up for a moment from the rush of your daily lives, you will hear the quiet voices of your country crying out for help," he stated. "You will see your reflection in the weary eyes of those who are losing hope in America. And you will see that our democracy is lying there in the gutter waiting for us to give it a second breath of life."[33]

Along the campaign trail, Gore often took the opportunity to speak out about the environment. He criticized the Bush administration's environmental record, and especially its reluctance to address the issue of global warming. Bush argued that forcing American industries to reduce their carbon dioxide emissions would be harmful to the U.S. economy. He and his vice president, Dan Quayle, ridiculed Gore for focusing on the issue. They and other Republicans characterized Gore's environmental views as radical and a threat to economic growth.

Gore responded to such criticism with strong words of his own:

> I believe that the extremist view is held by those who are willing to tolerate the doubling of carbon dioxide in a single generation, the loss in a single lifetime of more than half the living species God put on earth, the destruction of a large percentage of the protective ozone shield in only a few decades, the loss of more than an acre of tropical rain forest every second, the addition of an entire China's worth of people every decade, the poisoning of our air and water resources, the serious erosion of our cropland. Those of us who are attempting to rally this nation to lead a worldwide response to this crisis are responding in a common-sense way.[34]

President Bill Clinton

Bill Clinton was born as William Jefferson Blythe III on August 19, 1946, in Hope, Arkansas. He was named after his father, who had been killed in a car accident three months before his birth. His mother, Virginia Kelly, later married Roger Clinton, and Bill adopted his stepfather's last name.

Always an excellent student, Clinton became interested in a career in government during high school. As a delegate to the Boys Nation leadership program, he got to visit the White House and meet one of his heroes, President John F. Kennedy.

After earning a bachelor's degree in international affairs from Georgetown University in 1968, Clinton attended Oxford University in England for two years on a Rhodes Scholarship. He earned a law degree from Yale University in 1973.

Upon completing his education, Clinton returned to Arkansas and entered politics. Although he was narrowly defeated in his 1974 campaign for Congress, observers agreed that he was a gifted young politician. The following year Clinton married Hillary Rodham, whom he had met in law school. They eventually had a daughter, Chelsea.

Clinton was elected attorney general of Arkansas in 1976. Two years later, he became the youngest person ever to be elected governor of the state. Clinton failed to win a second term, but he returned to the governor's office in 1982 and served for the next ten years.

Throughout his years in Arkansas politics, Clinton was also active in the Democratic Party at the national level. After earning the party's presidential nomination in 1992, Clinton defeated Republican President George H.W. Bush and independent candidate Ross Perot to become the forty-second president of the United States. The nation enjoyed peace and economic prosperity under Clinton's leadership, and he was elected to a second term in office in 1996.

In 1998, following an investigation into his personal conduct, Clinton became the second president in history to be

continued

impeached. He was tried in the Senate, found not guilty, and allowed to remain in office. Clinton apologized to the American people and remained popular for the remainder of his term.

After leaving office in January 2001, Clinton remained active. He practiced law, gave speeches, and led fundraising campaigns to provide relief to hurricane victims. In 2004 he published a memoir called *My Life*. In 2008 he became a leading supporter of his wife's presidential campaign.

Becomes an Influential Vice President

The effectiveness of the Clinton-Gore campaign became clear on election day. They won the election by earning 43 percent of the popular vote, compared to 38 percent for Bush and 19 percent for independent candidate Ross Perot. Importantly, the Clinton-Gore ticket claimed several states in the South that the Democratic Party had not won in twenty-five years.

Gore was sworn in as the forty-fifth vice president of the United States on January 20, 1993. From the time he took office, he played a larger and more influential role than any other vice president in history. Gore set up an office very close to the president's Oval Office. The two men met for lunch every week to discuss policy issues. Gore helped Clinton choose officials to serve in his cabinet and to fill other important positions in the administration. He also attended dress rehearsals for Clinton's speeches and offered comments and criticism. The president relied on Gore's experience in Washington to help him get things done.

Overall, Gore became one of Clinton's closest and most trusted advisors. He managed to express his opinions without overstepping his authority. "My principal mission is to help Bill Clinton be the most successful president he can be," he explained. "The only time I speak up is when I feel that the President is not going to be well served by going in the direction that is recommended."[35]

Leads Effort to Reinvent Government

Gore also proved his value to the Clinton administration outside of the White House. For instance, in the spring of 1993 he took charge of an important program called the National Performance

Gore smashes an ashtray during a 1993 appearance on **The Late Show with David Letterman** *as part of a presentation on overly complicated and wasteful government purchasing regulations.*

Gore Represents the Administration on NAFTA

During his first term as vice president, Gore took a leading role in promoting the Clinton administration's position on the North American Free Trade Agreement (NAFTA). Clinton and his advisors supported this treaty, which would eliminate all major trading barriers between the United States and its closest neighbors, Canada and Mexico. They believed that free trade within North America would open new markets for American products and increase job and investment opportunities for American companies.

Critics of NAFTA, on the other hand, claimed that the agreement would encourage companies to send high-paying manufacturing jobs to lower-wage countries. The leading critic of NAFTA was Ross Perot, the outspoken, wealthy businessman who had attracted many supporters as an independent presidential candidate in the 1992 elections. In an effort to increase support for NAFTA among the American people, Gore agreed to debate Perot on the cable-television program *Larry King Live*.

During the debate, Gore refuted all of Perot's points and even made his opponent lose his temper. According to one biographer, "his strong performance and Perot's meltdown changed the dynamics of the NAFTA debate." Opinion polls showed that 33 percent of the American people opposed NAFTA before the debate, compared to 29 percent who favored it. Following the debate, however, the percentage of Americans who favored the treaty increased to 36 percent, while the percentage opposed decreased to 31 percent.

Gore, center, appears with Ross Perot, left, on CNN's Larry King Live in November 1993 to debate the details of the North American Free Trade Agreement (NAFTA).

Bill Turque, *Inventing Al Gore*. Boston: Houghton Mifflin, 2000, p. 285.

Review. Also known as Reinventing Government, the program identified sources of waste, fraud, and other abuse of taxpayers' money in the federal government. The idea behind the initiative was to downsize and streamline the government by eliminating unnecessary employees, simplifying complicated rules, and emphasizing customer service.

Gore and his team conducted an in-depth study of the inner workings of various government agencies, and they released their plan to make the federal government more efficient in September 1993. The report included 384 recommendations and promised $108 billion in savings. It called for eliminating 252,000 jobs, or 12 percent of the federal workforce, by 1998. Gore promoted the Reinventing Government initiative in a series of speeches and television appearances. In a memorable appearance on *The Late Show with David Letterman*, he performed a skit called "Stupid Government Tricks." The vice president shared real stories about the federal government's ridiculously complicated rules for purchasing commonplace items, such as regulations that caused the purchase price of the ashtray to increase from $4 to $54.

Some critics asserted that Gore's efforts to streamline the federal government avoided asking hard questions about the role of government and the need for various agencies and programs. But Gore argued that the Reinventing Government initiative produced some important recommendations. "If we can make these changes, we can create a government that works better and costs less,"[36] he declared. As it turned out, Gore's plan actually eliminated 330,000 jobs over the next five years, reducing the federal payroll by 15.4 percent to its smallest level since 1960.

Plays an Active Role

After completing the Reinventing Government initiative, Gore turned his attention to technology issues. He negotiated with television executives to develop a voluntary ratings system for TV programs. He also convinced manufacturers of TV sets to install V chips to enable parents to block children from viewing inappropriate programs. Building on his knowledge of the Internet, Gore also supervised the creation of a Web site for the White House that gave the American people a single point of access for government information.

Gore found his active role in the Clinton administration to be deeply rewarding. He claimed that his influence as vice president kept him from dwelling on what it would be like to be president himself. "I have never felt what so many vice presidents have reportedly felt: 'That should be me there.' Or 'I could do a lot better,'" he stated. "And I'm not spending any time or energy thinking about tomorrow and the ambition to be president. Some people might find that implausible, but that's the honest truth."[37]

In 1996 Clinton and Gore geared up for a re-election battle against Republican presidential nominee Bob Dole, a veteran senator from Kansas, and his vice presidential choice, Jack Kemp. The Clinton-Gore ticket enjoyed a comfortable lead in national polls for much of the 1996 presidential race. They ended up winning reelection by claiming 49.2 percent of the popular vote, compared to 40.7 percent for Dole and 8.4 percent for independent candidate Ross Perot.

Takes a Stand on the Environment

During Gore's second term as vice president in the Clinton administration, he helped secure an international agreement to address the problem of global warming. In 1996 the United Nations had released the results of a major study by the Intergovernmental Panel on Climate Change, a group of 2,500 leading scientists from 150 nations around the world. The study concluded that human activity—especially the rapid increase in emissions of carbon dioxide into the atmosphere—was causing alarming changes to the Earth's climate. It concluded that an international effort was needed to address the problem.

Following the release of the study, the United Nations organized a meeting of its member countries in Kyoto, Japan, in 1997 to forge an agreement on global climate change. As the Kyoto talks approached, though, Gore found himself caught

Gore leads a group visiting a lake near the Grinnell Glacier in Montana's Glacier National Park in September 1997 to illustrate his concerns about the effects of global warming.

in the middle of competing interests. Leaders of American business and industry pressured the Clinton administration to avoid strict limits on emissions that might be harmful to the U.S. economy. In the meantime, members of the environmental movement encouraged the administration to take a leading role in the negotiations.

As the Kyoto summit got underway, many nations expressed disappointment with the small changes proposed by the American representatives. Other countries were reluctant to make major changes on their own, so the discussions nearly collapsed shortly after they began. Fearing that the meeting would break up without producing an agreement, Gore decided to take action. Ignoring the advice of his staff, the vice president flew to Japan and personally joined in the talks. He started off by saying that the United States was prepared to show greater flexibility in discussing limits on carbon dioxide emissions. He also met privately with the representatives of several nations and demanded their cooperation in reaching a deal.

Gore's presence put the negotiations back on track and helped ensure that the parties reached an agreement to address global climate change. "It was the most courageous and important thing that Al Gore has ever done," said Greg Wetstone of the National Resources Defense Council. "He took the risk of personally going, inserting himself, and ultimately securing an intelligent agreement."[38] The Kyoto Protocol, as the agreement was called, never passed the U.S. Congress. It was eventually accepted by 180 other nations, however, so it remained an important achievement for Gore and the Clinton administration.

Remains Loyal during Clinton's Impeachment

The Clinton administration was credited with a number of other achievements. For example, the president passed an economic plan that paid off $360 billion of the national debt, balanced the federal budget, and paved the way for eight straight years of economic growth. The administration's policies helped to create

Gore defends his activities related to campaign fundraising to reporters in the White House press room in March 1997, after critics claimed that he had broken the law by making phone calls from his office to solicit donations to the Democratic Party.

twenty-two million new jobs, giving the nation its lowest unemployment rate in thirty years. American families benefited from the strong economy by earning higher incomes, paying lower taxes, and enjoying increased ownership of homes and participation in the stock market.

While Clinton was working toward these achievements, though, he faced persistent questions about his personal conduct. For instance, political opponents claimed that Clinton had extramarital affairs both before and after he became president. The most serious allegation charged that Clinton had a sexual relationship with a White House intern named Monica Lewinsky, then arranged for her to get a government job so that she would not reveal the affair.

The president denied the Lewinsky charges repeatedly: in a meeting with Gore and other administration officials; in a televised press conference; and in sworn testimony during a 1998 court case. A short time later, however, Lewinsky produced evidence that proved she and Clinton had a sexual relationship. The president was forced to admit that he had lied to cover up the affair. "I misled people, including even my wife," he said in a televised speech. "I deeply regret that."[39]

After a lengthy investigation into Clinton's personal life, independent counsel Kenneth Starr issued a report that included details of the president's sexual encounters with Lewinsky. Clinton's political opponents said that the report showed that he had committed the crimes of perjury (lying under oath to tell the truth) and obstruction of justice (interfering with an official investigation). In December 1998 the U.S. House of Representatives voted to impeach the president.

The U.S. Constitution allows for federal government officials to be impeached (charged with a crime) and removed from office if they are found guilty. The House of Representatives brings the criminal charges and acts as the prosecutor. The chief justice of the Supreme Court presides over the trial as a judge, and the Senate hears the case and votes as a jury. Two-thirds of the Senate must vote to convict in order to remove the impeached official from office.

Gore condemned the Republican-controlled Congress's decision to impeach the president. Although he felt that Clinton was wrong to have an affair and lie about it, he believed that the president's personal life should remain private. He claimed that Clinton's political opponents would use any excuse to remove him from office. "I do believe this is the saddest day I have seen in the nation's capital," he said following the House vote. "Invoking the solemn power of impeachment in the cause of partisan politics is wrong. What happened as a result does a great disservice to a man I believe will be regarded in the history book as one of our greatest presidents."[40]

Gore appears with President Bill Clinton to respond to the House of Representatives' impeachment vote in December 1998. Gore stood by Clinton throughout the investigations into the president's personal conduct and his impeachment trial.

Gore remained loyal to the president throughout the impeachment hearings, emphasizing his view that Clinton's affair was a personal rather than a political matter. Polls showed that a majority of Americans shared this view. Clinton's approval rating remained high during the Senate trial, which lasted for several weeks and generated a great deal of media coverage. When the Senate finally voted on February 12, 1999, Clinton was found not guilty and allowed to remain in office.

Gore praised the result of the trial and encouraged everyone to turn their attention back to the important issues facing the nation. "What the president did was terribly wrong; it was indefensible. He's apologized for it," he said in an interview. "And you know what the American people want? They want us to move on. They want us to focus on the future, and talk about them, and work on their problems, and build their future, not wallow in the past."[41]

Chapter 5

The 2000 Election

Following eight years as an active and influential vice president, Al Gore ran for president in 2000. The contest between him and Republican nominee George W. Bush turned out to be one of the closest and most controversial elections in American history. After a series of recounts and legal battles that lasted for five weeks, the results of the disputed election were finally decided by the U.S. Supreme Court.

Launches 2000 Presidential Campaign

After serving two terms as vice president in the Clinton administration, Gore decided to run for president in the 2000 election. He formally announced his candidacy on June 15, 1999. Like every other campaign in his political career, Gore launched his bid for the presidency from the steps of the Smith County courthouse in Carthage, Tennessee. Even before he made it official, however, many people already viewed him as the front-runner for the Democratic Party nomination.

Under normal circumstances, the sitting vice president in a successful administration is in a strong position to become the next president. The vice president is familiar to voters, has experience helping to run the country, and usually enjoys the support of his political party. Although these factors worked in Gore's favor, his association with the Clinton administration also had some negative effects on his candidacy.

Clinton's impeachment proceedings had concluded just four months before Gore launched his presidential campaign. The president's many achievements and the nation's prosperity ensured that Clinton remained popular in some quarters. But many Americans disapproved of the scandals and ugly partisan bickering that had characterized much of his time in office. Political analysts wondered how this general feeling would affect Gore's presidential hopes.

Gore thus found himself in a tricky position as he launched his campaign. On the one hand, he wanted to take credit for his role in the Clinton administration's successful policies and the strong U.S. economy they helped create. "It's certainly not going to be one of my priorities to try to manufacture some differences in policy and approaches, because I'm very proud of the role that I've played in helping President Clinton shape this administration,"[42] he stated. On the other hand, Gore wanted to distance himself from doubts about the president's personal behavior and morality. In the area of personal character, Gore tried to emphasize his own reputation for honesty, integrity, and strong moral values.

Gore's Opponents

Gore's only significant opponent for the Democratic presidential nomination was Senator Bill Bradley of New Jersey. Bradley ran a thoughtful, positive campaign, but he could not overcome Gore's advantages in visibility and party support. As expected, Gore easily earned the Democratic Party nomination.

Meanwhile, the winner of the Republican Party nomination was George W. Bush. He was the eldest son of former president George H.W. Bush and the two-term governor of Texas, the second-largest state in the country. These factors enabled Bush to build a broad base of support within the Republican Party and amass a huge campaign fund.

Bush cruised to an easy victory over his main rival, Senator John McCain of Arizona, in the state primary elections. After receiving the Republican nomination, Bush selected Dick Cheney as his vice presidential running mate. Cheney had served as secretary of defense in the George H.W. Bush administration. He was regarded as a level-headed, reliable, conservative politician who brought strong foreign-policy experience to the campaign.

The 2000 campaign also featured a third-party candidate, attorney and political activist Ralph Nader. Nader was best known for his criticism of large corporations and his work to protect American consumers. As the presidential nominee of the Green Party, Nader attracted support from voters who wanted reform and were not pleased with either of the major-party candidates.

Campaign Issues

In the early part of the campaign, Gore tried to emphasize the differences between himself and his opponents on important issues. Some of his priorities included improving the nation's public schools, expanding health care benefits for children and families, protecting the environment in ways that would create jobs, and passing laws to make political campaign fundraising more open and fair.

While Gore outlined his policy positions, it became clear that many voters were more concerned about other issues. For example,

Democratic presidential candidate Gore and his running mate, Senator Joe Lieberman, wave to supporters in Tennessee during their campaign for the White House in 2000.

polls showed that many people were worried about what they viewed as a decline in moral values in American society. They felt that the media and popular culture promoted permissive attitudes toward sex, abortion, and homosexuality. They wanted to elect a candidate who would put an end to scandals in Washington, restore integrity to the presidency, and guide the country back onto a solid moral path.

Throughout the campaign, Bush portrayed himself as a reformer who had not been tainted by Washington politics. He emphasized his religious faith, his support for abstinence programs, and his opposition to abortion and gay rights. He also proposed to use the federal budget to fund tax cuts or tax refunds. These positions had a great deal of appeal to conservative voters.

As the Democratic National Convention approached, Gore trailed Bush in the national polls. Some of Gore's advisors felt that the vice president's campaign was being harmed by voters' doubts about Clinton's character and values. They encouraged Gore to distance himself from the president and establish himself as an independent thinker.

Gore turned this advice into action at the convention. First, he selected Senator Joseph Lieberman of Connecticut as his vice presidential running mate. Lieberman was the first Jewish American ever to be nominated for the position by a major political party, and he had also been the first Democratic member of Congress to condemn Clinton's behavior during the Monica Lewinsky scandal. Many observers viewed Gore's selection of Lieberman as a bold choice. Gore also emphasized the healthy state of his own marriage by giving his wife a long, passionate kiss on stage at the convention. Finally, Gore proclaimed his independence in his acceptance speech upon receiving the nomination. "I stand here tonight my own man, and I want you to know me for who I truly am,"[43] he declared.

Image Problems

Despite these actions, however, Gore suffered from a growing image problem. Many voters had come to view him as stiff, dull, arrogant, and obsessed with detail. In many cases, the media coverage of his campaign seemed to reinforce these ideas. Political

The Electoral College

The confusing results of the 2000 presidential election put the electoral college in the national spotlight. The electoral college is a system for electing the president of the United States that is described in the U.S. Constitution. It was originally put in place because the framers of the Constitution disagreed about how the president should be chosen. Some wanted the American people to vote for president directly, while others wanted Congress to select the president. They came up with the electoral college system as a compromise between these two methods. Under this system, the citizens of each state vote for president, and the winner of each state's election receives a number of electoral votes. The candidate who receives a majority of all available electoral votes wins the election.

On election day, eligible voters go to local polling places to cast ballots for the candidate they want to be president. This part of the process is called the popular vote. Al Gore received the highest popular vote total in 2000, but this did not mean he won the election. The electoral college is the second step in the election process. Each state chooses people to serve in the electoral college, called electors. The number of electors for each state is equal to the size of its congressional delegation: two senators, plus a number of representatives that varies based on the state's population. Larger states have more congressional representatives, and thus receive more electors. In 2000, California had the most electoral votes with 54, followed by New York (33), Texas (32), and Florida (25). Several states with small populations had the minimum number of 3, including Alaska, Delaware, and Montana.

A few weeks after a presidential election, the electors for each state meet to cast their votes for president. The electors almost always vote for the candidate who won the popular vote in their state, although only about half of the states have laws requiring them to do so. In order to become president, a candidate must receive a majority of the available electoral votes. There were 538

continued

total electoral votes available in the 2000 election, so a minimum of 270 were needed to win. After Bush was declared the winner of the popular vote in Florida, he was awarded that state's 25 electoral votes, giving him a total of 271 and the presidency. If neither candidate had received a majority, the U.S. House of Representatives would have chosen the next president from among the top vote getters.

commentators often focused on Gore's mannerisms and motivations rather than his policy positions. "The default position on Al Gore appears to be ridicule," political analyst Joe Klein wrote. "He opens his mouth and is immediately assumed cynical, tactical, self-serving, self-pitying, awkward, embarrassing, unintentionally hilarious, or all of the above."[44]

Republican presidential candidate George W. Bush makes a point during a debate with Gore at Washington University in October 2000. Reporters and voters often contrasted Bush's easygoing, likable style with Gore's public persona, which was seen as stiff and awkward.

In comparison to Gore, Bush received fairly positive media coverage of his personality and image. Reporters who followed his campaign often described the Republican candidate as easy-going, informal, straightforward, and sincere. They generally presented Bush as a likeable fellow, which helped him overcome some voters' concerns about his intelligence and qualifications.

Gore changed his campaign strategy several times in an attempt to connect with voters. He tried to shift the emphasis away from his personality and toward his experience. He argued that it was more important for the president of the United States to be well prepared than to be well liked. But Gore's message continued to be muffled by the media's negative portrayals of his personality.

The 2000 Election

After months of intensive campaigning by both Gore and Bush, American voters finally went to the polls on November 7, 2000, to elect the next president. As soon as the returns began coming in, it became clear that the election results would be extremely close. The Gore-Lieberman ticket did very well in the Northeast, winning every state but New Hampshire. They also performed well in the Upper Midwest—winning in Illinois, Michigan, Minnesota, and Wisconsin—and in states along the West Coast. In the meantime, the Bush-Cheney ticket carried the South (including Gore's home state of Tennessee) and Southwest, as well as the Rocky Mountain states and the rural midwestern farming states.

By the time the polls closed, Gore led Bush by more than 500,000 votes nationwide. Under the U.S. Constitution, however, presidential elections are not decided by the total number of votes cast for each candidate. Instead, the popular vote totals within each state are used to determine which candidate will earn that state's electoral votes. The candidate who wins the majority of the state electoral votes, rather than the majority of the national popular vote, becomes the next president.

There were a total of 538 electoral votes available in the 2000 election, so either Gore or Bush needed to earn a minimum of 270 to win. After tight contests were decided in several other states, the result of the entire election came down to the state of Florida. Not counting Florida, Gore had earned 267 electoral votes—3 short of the number he needed to win the presidency—while Bush had earned 246. The candidate who prevailed in Florida would earn that state's 25 electoral votes and the victory.

Controversial Recounts in Florida

Unfortunately for both candidates, the election results in Florida remained in dispute for several weeks. On the night of the election, the television networks originally projected that Gore had won in Florida. They based this prediction on exit polls, or surveys taken as voters left their local polling places.

Later that night, once some of the actual votes had been counted, the television networks reversed their earlier projec-

The headlines on four editions of the Orlando Sentinel *issued on November 8, 2000, track the uncertain results of the presidential election between Gore and George W. Bush.*

tion and declared Bush the winner in Florida. At this point, Gore called Bush on the telephone to concede, or admit defeat. As it turned out, however, the early election returns had not included some counties that typically favored Democratic candidates, such as Broward, Miami-Dade, Palm Beach, and Volusia. The returns from these counties narrowed the gap between Bush and Gore considerably. The television networks then retracted their earlier claims that Bush had taken Florida and informed viewers that the election results were too close to call. Gore called Bush again to withdraw his concession until all of the votes were counted.

On the morning of November 8, the tally in Florida showed Bush ahead by 1,784 votes statewide, out of a total of more than 5.8 million cast. Under state law, such a close election result triggered an automatic machine recount. This meant that all of the paper ballots were fed through voting machines a second time to verify the results. Following this machine recount, Bush's lead decreased to 327 votes.

Florida law also allows the candidates involved in extremely close elections to request further recounts to be performed by hand. Gore asked for hand recounts to be performed in four Florida counties. As soon as the hand counting of ballots began, though, many people raised concerns about the fairness of the process.

The Florida counties in question used punch-card ballots that could be confusing for voters. The idea was that voters would punch out a perforated area, known as a chad, to make a hole next to the name of their preferred candidate for president. Then the ballots were fed into machines that read the holes and recorded the votes. But many voters seemed to have trouble with this system. Many election observers expressed concern that the confusing layout of the ballots may have caused Gore supporters to accidentally vote for independent candidate Pat Buchanan. In addition, the hand recounts revealed thousands of ballots with incompletely punched holes. Such inconclusive holes became known as dimpled or pregnant chads (areas that were indented but not punched out) and hanging chads (areas that were punched through but still attached). Many other ballots incorrectly showed marks for two candidates (known as overvotes) or no candidates (undervotes).

The voting machines that had initially read the ballots simply threw out any that had been punched out incorrectly. During the hand recounts, however, it became clear that these uncounted ballots could determine the outcome of the election. The county officials who led the recount efforts struggled to decide whether and how to count these confusing ballots. Many people worried that the officials—influenced by their own political beliefs—might adjust the counting standards to favor one candidate or the other. As a result, the hand recounting process became extremely controversial. Adding to the stress and anxiety of the situation, the county offices where the hand recounts took place were surrounded by television cameras and protesters.

The hand recounts went on around the clock in an effort to beat a deadline. Florida law required the secretary of state to certify the results of an election within seven days. The person who held that office in 2000, Katherine Harris, was a Republican who had served as cochair of George W. Bush's campaign in the state. In addition, the governor of Florida at that time was Bush's younger brother, Jeb Bush. As the deadline approached, the counties asked Harris for an extension to give them time to complete the hand recounts. Harris denied the requests and declared her intention to certify the election results, with Bush as the winner, as scheduled on November 15. Many Gore supporters—and some independent observers—condemned her decision and accused her of acting in a biased manner.

Bush v. Gore

The heated controversy surrounding the Florida recounts soon ended up in court. On November 17, the Florida Supreme Court issued an injunction (court order) to prevent Harris from certifying the election results. Five days later, the justices ruled that the hand recounts should be included in the final tally and established a new deadline of November 26 for the counties to complete the process.

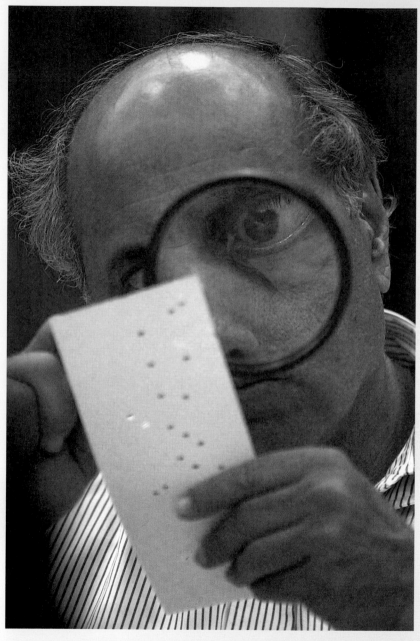

Judge Robert Rosenberg examines a ballot in Broward County, Florida, as part of the controversial vote recounts in that state in the wake of uncertain presidential election results in November 2000.

Bush immediately appealed this ruling to the U.S. Supreme Court, which agreed to hear oral arguments in the case of *Bush v. Gore* on December 1. Bush's position was that the hand recounts were not being handled consistently or fairly, so they should not be included in the final tally. He also claimed that the justices of the Florida Supreme Court—who had all been appointed by Democratic governors—had no authority to overturn state election laws and invent a new system for determining election results.

While the U.S. Supreme Court prepared to hear the case, Harris certified the Florida election results on the new deadline of November 26. At that point, the official tally—which included some previously uncounted absentee ballots—showed Bush as the winner by 537 votes. The following day, Gore formally contested the results. In a nationally televised address, he told the American people that he wanted a complete and accurate count of all the votes cast in Florida, no matter how long it took to complete. He argued that ensuring fair election results was vital to preserving America's democratic system of government.

On December 4, the U.S. Supreme Court issued its ruling on Bush's appeal. The justices unanimously agreed to return the case to the Florida Supreme Court. They asked the state court to clarify or reconsider its decision to extend the deadline for manual recounts. Many observers interpreted this ruling as a strong suggestion that the Florida Supreme Court should stop interfering in the election process and allow the results to stand. On the same day, Florida Judge N. Sanders Sauls rejected Gore's legal effort to contest Harris's certification of the election results. Sauls said that he found no evidence to support Gore's claims that more recounting would change the outcome of the election.

At this point, things did not look good for Gore. He had come out on the losing end of two legal decisions in a row, and it appeared likely that the election results would stand. On December 8, however, the Florida Supreme Court stepped in to give Gore hope again. At the request of the U.S. Supreme Court, the justices had reconsidered their earlier ruling granting more time to complete hand recounts. Instead of deciding that ruling had been wrong, though, the Florida Supreme Court decided that it had not gone far enough. The justices ordered hand recounts of all undervotes to begin immediately across the state. "The turn of events that evening was stunning," one analyst noted. "Gore, all but out of the running, was revived, and not only revived, but thought likely to win the election."[45]

The U.S. Supreme Court Ends the Election

Gore's last chance for victory did not last long, however. The following day, the U.S. Supreme Court ordered all recounts to stop until it could hear Bush's appeal of the Florida Supreme Court ruling. The oral arguments took place on December 11, and the justices issued their ruling the next day. By a 7-2 vote, they found the system of recounting votes in Florida to be unconstitutional. They said that the many different standards used to count votes—and the arbitrary ways in which those standards had been chosen—violated the Equal Protection Clause of the Fourteenth Amendment to the U.S. Constitution, which states that laws must apply to every citizen in the same way.

After finding the Florida recount methods unconstitutional, the Court considered legal remedies, or potential ways to fix the situation. The justices were split on this question, but the conservative majority on the Court prevailed by a 5-4 vote. The majority ruled that it was not possible for Florida to recount the votes in a constitutional way by December 12. This date was the deadline established in the U.S. Constitution for states to choose electors for the electoral college. If Florida did not choose electors by the deadline, it would forfeit its twenty-five electoral votes.

Four of the nine justices disagreed with this part of the decision and issued dissenting opinions to explain their reasoning. Justice John Paul Stevens argued that the Court was wrong to halt the recounting of votes in Florida. He felt that the decision was politically motivated, and thus could undermine the American people's respect for the democratic process. "Preventing the recount from being completed will inevitably cast a cloud on the legitimacy of the election," Stevens wrote. "Although we may never know with complete certainty the identity of the winner of this year's presidential election, the identity of the loser is perfectly clear. It is the nation's confidence in the judge as an impartial guardian of the rule of law."[46]

Decision Sparks Criticism

The U.S. Supreme Court decision in *Bush v. Gore* effectively ended all recounting in Florida and allowed the earlier results to stand. Bush received Florida's electoral votes, giving him a total of 271 and making him the next president of the United States. Gore became only the third presidential candidate in American history to win the popular vote but lose the election (this also happened in the elections of 1876 and 1888).

Many people criticized the Court's decision to end the recounts and hand the election to Bush. Some critics claimed that the five conservative justices who made up the majority had ruled in favor of Bush because they shared his political beliefs. These critics called the decision biased, corrupt, and a violation of judicial responsibility. They said that the Supreme Court had stolen the presidency from Gore. "*Bush v. Gore* will go down in history as one of the worst decisions the Supreme Court ever made," wrote President Bill Clinton."[47]

On the other hand, many Americans supported the Court's decision to step in and end the election dispute. Some believed that it was impossible to recount the votes in a way that would be considered fair to all parties. They felt that the best solution was to allow the results of the original machine recount to stand. Others had simply grown tired of all the controversy surrounding the election. They wanted to pick a new president and move on to address the important issues facing the nation.

Gore Accepts Defeat

Although Gore strongly disagreed with the U.S. Supreme Court's ruling, he decided that accepting it was in the best interest of the country. On December 13, he once again called Bush to concede, and this time he promised not to call back. Later that evening, Gore made a nationally televised concession speech. He encour-

Gore Concedes to Bush

On December 13, 2000, shortly after the U.S. Supreme Court announced its decision to halt the recounting of votes in Florida, Gore officially admitted defeat in the presidential election. His nationally televised concession speech is excerpted below:

Just moments ago, I spoke with George W. Bush and congratulated him on becoming the 43rd president of the United States. . . .

I say to President-elect Bush that what remains of partisan rancor must now be put aside, and may God bless his stewardship of this country.

Neither he nor I anticipated this long and difficult road. Certainly neither of us wanted it to happen. Yet it came, and now it has ended, resolved, as it must be resolved, through the honored institutions of our democracy. . . .

Now the U.S. Supreme Court has spoken. Let there be no doubt, while I strongly disagree with the court's decision, I accept it. I accept the finality of this outcome which will be ratified next Monday in the Electoral College. And tonight, for the sake of our unity of the people and the strength of our democracy, I offer my concession.

I also accept my responsibility, which I will discharge unconditionally, to honor the new president-elect and do everything possible to help him bring Americans together in fulfillment of the great vision that our Declaration of Independence defines and that our Constitution affirms and defends. . . .

I know that many of my supporters are disappointed. I am too. But our disappointment must be overcome by our love of country. . . .

continued

And while there will be time enough to debate our continuing differences, now is the time to recognize that that which unites us is greater than that which divides us.

While we yet hold and do not yield our opposing beliefs, there is a higher duty than the one we owe to political party. This is America and we put country before party. We will stand together behind our new president.

Al Gore, "Vice President Al Gore Delivers Remarks," *CNN.com*, December 13, 2000. http://www.cnn.com/ELECTION/2000/transcripts/121300/t651213.html.

aged the American people to put the election controversy behind them and unite in support of the new president.

Bush also appeared on television to give an acceptance speech. The new president-elect thanked Gore for being gracious in defeat and expressed eagerness to move forward. He also promised to work hard to heal the divisions that the election dispute had created.

By the time the controversy finally ended, America and the world had waited five long weeks to find out who would become the next president of the United States. Many observers marveled at the peaceful transition of power that took place following such a long and bitter struggle. Some people felt that it was a testament to the strength of American democracy. "The 2000 presidential election reflected American politics in all its high drama," acknowledged one analyst. "But Americans did not worry needlessly about the outcome. They knew there would be no military coup, no UN peacekeeping force, no new election. They knew, rather, that in time there would be a winner, a transition, and an inauguration."[48]

After Bush took office on January 20, 2001, several news organizations conducted their own independent recounts of the disputed Florida ballots. The results varied depending on the

Gore greets President-elect George W. Bush outside of the vice president's residence in December 2000 after earlier conceding the controversial election to the Republican candidate.

recount methods used. Some methods confirmed a Bush victory and others indicated that Gore would have won. In order to avoid such confusion in the future, both state and federal governments considered various election reform measures. Some of the suggested changes included redesigning ballots to make them easier to use and installing modern electronic voting equipment.

Chapter 6

Champion of the Environment

The terrible disappointment of the 2000 presidential election marked the end of Al Gore's career in politics. After returning to life as a private citizen, he decided to focus his energy on raising public awareness of the threat of global climate change. With the release of the award-winning 2006 documentary film *An Inconvenient Truth*, Gore emerged as one of the world's leading environmental activists. In 2007 he received the prestigious Nobel Peace Prize for his efforts to combat global warming.

Becomes a Private Citizen

Once President George W. Bush took office in January 2001, Gore's twenty-five-year career in public service came to an end. Although Gore acknowledged that the controversial outcome was difficult for him to take, he refused to discuss his views on the election. Instead, he expressed his desire to put the painful defeat in the past and move forward.

For the first few months after he left office, Gore withdrew from the public eye. He and his wife, Tipper, moved from Washington back to Nashville. They reconnected with old friends and worked on a book together about the American family. That summer the Gores spent time in southern Spain and sailed along the coast of Greece. Gore relaxed, enjoyed good food and beautiful scenery, and grew a full beard.

A bearded Gore speaks at a Democratic Party fundraiser in Nashville, Tennessee, in February 2002, after spending much of his time upon leaving public office the previous year out of the public eye.

As Gore gradually recovered his spirits, he considered various options for a future career. He received numerous offers to teach college classes as a visiting professor, and he accepted positions at Columbia University, Fisk University, Middle Tennessee State University, and the University of California at Los Angeles (UCLA). He also became a senior advisor to the fast-growing Internet search company Google in 2001, and he joined the board of directors at Apple Computer in 2003.

In 2004 Gore became a partner in a new business venture called Generation Investment Management. Based in London, England, the firm invests clients' money in companies that operate in ways that benefit society and the environment. Gore made a special effort to support companies that seemed well-prepared to deal with global warming. He believed that these companies would perform well as the climate crisis worsened and the world's governments were forced to place stricter controls on pollution.

As Gore immersed himself in business and technology, many people were impressed by his ability to understand issues, identify trends, and spot future opportunities. "His new work leverages what he's really good at, which is thinking deeply about the drivers of change and having a perspective on where companies need to go in a global business environment,"[49] explained his friend and business partner Peter Knight.

Emerges as a Critic of Government

Gore also used his new perspective as a private citizen to think deeply about the challenges facing America's democratic system of government. In the first year after leaving office, Gore was careful to avoid making political statements. He seemed to want to remain on the sidelines in order to give the country time to heal from the divisive 2000 election. Gore generally refrained from criticizing the Bush administration during this time. Following the terrorist attacks of September 11, 2001, in fact, he expressed support for the president and called for national unity.

As time passed, though, Gore once again began expressing his opinion about important issues facing the country. He was particularly vocal in his opposition to Bush's decision to invade Iraq in 2003. Bush justified this decision by claiming that Iraq possessed weapons of mass destruction that could be used to

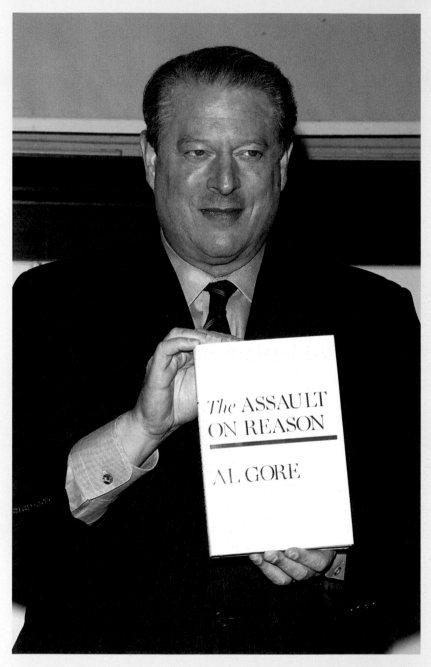

Gore displays a copy of his book, The Assault on Reason, a critical assessment of the state of democracy in America, at a book signing in May 2007.

arm terrorist groups. Administration officials also suggested that Iraqi leader Saddam Hussein was connected to the September 11 attacks.

Gore pointed out that there was very little evidence to support these claims. He accused the Bush administration of misleading the American people about its reasons for going to war. He argued that by starting a war under false pretenses, the president risked ruining America's reputation in the world. "I genuinely think he did a good job in the immediate aftermath of September 11," Gore said of Bush's performance. "Up until the invasion of Iraq, I think he did a good job. But then he blew it, in my opinion."[50]

As Gore spoke out against the Iraq War and other Bush administration policies, many Democratic Party supporters tried to convince him to run for president again in 2004. Some people who favored his candidacy proposed the campaign slogan "Re-elect Gore," referring to their belief that he had been cheated out of the presidency in 2000. Before the 2004 presidential campaign even got underway, however, Gore announced that he would not run against Bush. He worried that his candidacy would make the election center around events of the past rather than important issues. After deciding not to run, Gore donated $6 million left over from his 2000 campaign to various Democratic Party groups.

Although he chose to stay out of politics, Gore continued to observe the workings of government with great interest. He grew increasingly concerned about what he viewed as major failures of the democratic process. In the months leading up to the Iraq War, for instance, he felt that Congress, the news media, and the American people did not ask tough questions and demand adequate answers about the Bush administration's policies.

Gore eventually published a book, *The Assault on Reason*, outlining his concerns about American democracy.

> Faith in the power of reason—the belief that free citizens can govern themselves wisely and fairly by resorting to logical debate on the basis of the best evidence available, instead of raw power—was and remains the central premise of American democracy. This premise is now under

assault. The truth is that American democracy is now in danger—not from any one set of ideas, but from unprecedented changes in the environment within which ideas either live and spread, or wither and die. I do not mean the physical environment; I mean what is called the public sphere, or the marketplace of ideas.[51]

Gore also became involved in a business venture that he hoped would address some of the problems he identified. He and several partners launched an independent cable television network called Current TV. The network featured short video news segments that were submitted by young viewers across the country. It was designed to give ordinary people greater access to television, so that they would have an opportunity to publicize their ideas and participate in the democratic process. "He's a visionary," said Joel Hyatt, one of Gore's partners in the cable network. "He's doing things that are new, daring, difficult, just as he tried to do as a public servant."[52]

Becomes a Champion of the Environment

Gore's boldest undertaking after leaving office, however, was his all-out effort to sound an alarm about the threat of global climate change. Gore had first become interested in global warming as a student at Harvard in 1969, when he took a science course taught by Professor Roger Revelle. He had made several attempts to raise public awareness of the issue over the course of his political career. As a member of Congress in the 1980s, for instance, he had sponsored hearings about global climate change. He also addressed the topic in his 1992 book *Earth in the Balance*. As vice president, Gore had traveled to Kyoto, Japan, to help secure an international agreement to reduce carbon dioxide emissions that contribute to global warming.

Following Gore's defeat in the 2000 election, his wife had encouraged him to focus his energies on something he felt passionate about. He took Tipper's advice and began updating an

The Link Between the Climate Crisis and World Peace

Al Gore and the scientists of the Intergovernmental Panel on Climate Change (IPCC) shared the 2007 Nobel Peace Prize for their efforts to raise awareness of global warming and encourage people to address the climate crisis. When they were announced as the winners of the prestigious award, some people questioned how global warming related to world peace.

In response to this question, the Nobel committee explained that the human consequences of climate change could lead to violent conflicts. If the world steadily grew hotter and drier, for instance, people would likely have trouble finding water and growing food. This situation would create competition for scarce resources and increase the potential for war. By working to prevent the negative impacts of climate change from taking place, the committee noted, Gore and the IPCC thus helped to prevent future wars and promote peace.

old slide show presentation about global warming that he had created to accompany *Earth in the Balance*. Gore added recent data, improved the flow of the presentation, and used modern software to computerize it. Then, in 2002, he started traveling around the country and giving lectures about global warming.

Gore made his presentation hundreds of times over the next few years. It soon became clear that the slide show had a dramatic effect on audiences. Many people cried when confronted with the alarming facts and figures about global climate change. Many others approached Gore and offered to help him with his mission. Gore ended up training more than one thousand volunteers to give the lecture around the world.

An Inconvenient Truth

One person who was deeply impressed by Gore's global-warming presentation was the influential film producer Laurie David. She arranged for Gore to meet with Davis Guggenheim, an accomplished documentary filmmaker, about turning the slide show into a movie. Although Gore was doubtful at first, Guggenheim eventually convinced him that he could turn the material into a powerful film.

This film, called *An Inconvenient Truth*, was released on May 24, 2006. It was a huge hit at several major film festivals, getting standing ovations from audiences and winning a number of awards. It went on to earn $50 million at the box office and to sell more than 1.5 million copies on DVD.

An Inconvenient Truth combines footage from Gore's global-warming presentation with background information about his life. On the personal side, it shows the major turning points that contributed to Gore's transformation from politician to environmental activist. Throughout the interviews and speeches that are featured in the film, Gore discusses his life experiences and crusade to solve the climate crisis in an engaging, witty, and passionate way.

On the issue of global warming, the film presents scientific evidence of a link between the burning of carbon-based fossil fuels like coal, oil, and natural gas and a steady increase in average global temperatures. The burning of fossil fuels for energy releases carbon dioxide—an invisible, odorless, tasteless gas—into the Earth's atmosphere. Carbon dioxide is known as a greenhouse gas because it acts like the roof of a greenhouse to hold in heat from the sun. Some trapping of heat in the atmosphere is necessary to maintain a habitable temperature on the planet's surface. But Gore argues that human activity has led to a dramatic increase in carbon dioxide emissions in recent decades. He claims that this increase threatens to raise the average temperature on Earth to dangerous levels.

An Inconvenient Truth outlines many possible consequences of global warming. For example, increasing temperatures may melt glaciers and polar ice caps, which would cause sea levels to rise and trigger flooding of low-lying coastal areas around the world.

Gore appears in his Oscar-winning documentary An Inconvenient Truth, *a 2006 film adaptation of a presentation on global warming that he began delivering as a slide show in the 1980s while he was a member of Congress.*

In addition, changing ocean temperatures and currents could cause an increase in severe weather, including storms, droughts, and heat waves. Changing climate conditions could also force millions of species of plants and animals to shift their habitat or face extinction. An increase in worldwide temperatures could also allow epidemics of infectious diseases to spread from tropical regions to new places.

An Inconvenient Truth presents many frightening projections about the future of the planet. It also includes harsh criticism of the Bush administration, which Gore accuses of ignoring the climate crisis. But the film also offers hope for the future. It ends with a series of positive suggestions for viewers to reduce their personal carbon footprint, such as using compact fluorescent lightbulbs, taking mass transit, adjusting their thermostats to use less energy, and planting trees.

Unwilling to ask ordinary Americans to make sacrifices that he was unwilling to make himself, Gore adopted a carbon-neutral lifestyle. He updated his Nashville home to make it more energy efficient, for instance, and paid extra to obtain all of his electricity from renewable energy sources. To minimize the impact of his frequent travels around the world, Gore always flew on commercial airlines and purchased carbon offsets to make up for the pollution generated. (Carbon offset providers sell the greenhouse gas reductions associated with projects like wind farms to customers who want to offset the emissions they caused by flying, driving, or using electricity.)

Changes People's Minds

Before the release of An Inconvenient Truth, these measures seemed not only inconvenient, but also unnecessary to many Americans. Some doubted that global warming was occurring, while many others were unaware of its potential impacts. The movie—and the publicity that surrounded it—helped raise public awareness of the problem.

Many viewers found An Inconvenient Truth deeply affecting. After watching Gore make his case with scientific evidence, they became

*Gore poses with his Oscar in Hollywood, California, after
An Inconvenient Truth won the Academy Award for
Best Documentary Feature in February 2007. The film
is credited with increasing public awareness of the problem
of global warming.*

convinced of the need to address the climate crisis. "In tandem with Hurricane Katrina and a rising chorus of warning from climate scientists, Gore's film helped trigger one of the most dramatic opinion shifts in history as Americans suddenly realized they must change the way they live,"[53] noted one writer. Gore found it gratifying to see his message finally get through. "I feel like the country singer who spends 30 years on the road to become an overnight sensation," he noted. "And I've seen public interest wax and wane before—but this time does feel different."[54]

The impact of *An Inconvenient Truth* increased in early 2007, when it was honored with an Academy Award for Best Documentary Feature. At the Academy Awards ceremony, Gore appeared on stage with the director and crew to accept the award. He used the occasion as an opportunity to stress the importance of his mission. "My fellow Americans, people all over the world, we need to solve the climate crisis," he stated. "It's not a political issue, it's a moral issue. We have everything we need to get started, with the possible exception of the will to act. That's a renewable resource. Let's renew it."[55]

Doubters and Critics

The success of *An Inconvenient Truth* turned Gore into the most prominent activist in the fight against global warming. His status as the leader of the movement to address the climate crisis also made Gore the main target of criticism for people who disagreed with his position. Some critics—especially those with ties to industries that emitted large amounts of carbon dioxide—spent a great deal of time and money trying to discredit Gore's work.

Some people disputed Gore's claim that human activity was primarily responsible for increases in worldwide average temperatures. They argued that the trend toward higher global temperatures was part of a natural cycle that had caused both ice ages and periods of warming in the past. Other critics acknowledged that human activity contributed to global warming, but they claimed that Gore greatly exaggerated the potential impacts of the problem.

Pushes for Government Action

Such doubts only encouraged Gore to work harder to convince governments, industries, and individuals to take action to address the climate crisis. In March 2007 he traveled to Washington, D.C., to testify before Congress about global warming. He laid out an aggressive program for the United States to reduce its carbon dioxide emissions, which were the highest of any country in the world. Gore proposed an immediate freeze on emissions, followed by a series of reductions over time. He also suggested raising fuel economy standards for cars, banning the construction of new power plants that did not feature ways to capture and store pollution, and instituting a carbon tax on industries. Gore acknowledged that these proposals would encounter resistance, but he insisted that the environmental and economic cost of ignoring the climate crisis would be far worse.

Gore recognized that the U.S. government was more likely to adopt measures to address global warming if it faced intense political pressure from the American people. With that in mind, Gore founded the Alliance for Climate Protection, a bipartisan nonprofit organization, to help make the climate crisis an urgent political issue. The organization sponsored a huge Internet, TV, and print advertising campaign designed to encourage changes in consumer and business behavior and force shifts in government policy. As part of this effort, the alliance sponsored the Live Earth benefit concerts. These concerts—featuring a variety of big-name musical artists playing at stadiums around the world—took place on July 7, 2007.

Wins the Nobel Peace Prize

On October 12, 2007, Gore learned that he had been selected as a winner of the Nobel Peace Prize. He shared this prestigious honor with the United Nations' Intergovernmental Panel on Climate Change (IPCC), a group of leading scientists headed by Rajendra K. Pachauri of India. The prize committee bestowed the award on Gore and the IPCC for "their efforts to build up and disseminate greater knowledge about man-made climate change, and to lay

Gore, left, stands with fellow Nobel laureate Rajendra Pachauri at the ceremony in Oslo, Norway, that honored both men with the Nobel Peace Prize in December 2007 for their work to publicize and combat climate change.

the foundations for the measures that are needed to counteract that change."[56] The announcement praised the IPCC for its scientific research into the causes and consequences of global warming and Gore for his efforts to publicize that information. It described Gore as "the single individual who has done most to create greater worldwide understanding of the measures that need to be adopted."[57]

Gore accepted the Nobel Peace Prize on December 10, 2007. Although he appreciated the recognition of his efforts, he insisted that his mission was far from completed.

It's the greatest honor I could ever have, but it's hard to celebrate recognition of an effort that thus far has failed. I'm not finished, but thus far, I have failed. We have all failed. Today we're dumping 70 million tons of global-warming pollution into the environment, and tomorrow we will dump more, and there is no effective worldwide response. Until we start sharply reducing global-warming pollution, I will feel that I have failed.[58]

The international recognition Gore received did not seem to have much effect on his opponent in the disputed 2000 election. President Bush released a statement saying that he was happy for Gore. Bush insisted, however, that he did not feel any increased pressure to adopt measures to reduce America's carbon dioxide emissions. As a way of continuing his mission, Gore donated his share of the $1.5 million Nobel Peace Prize to the Alliance for Climate Protection.

Efforts to Draft as Presidential Candidate

Gore's high-profile role as an environmental crusader earned the admiration and respect of millions of people around the world. Many supporters urged him to build upon his success by running for president in 2008. One group of supporters even placed a full-page advertisement in the *New York Times* in an effort to convince Gore to run. "Your country needs you now, as do your party and the planet you are fighting so hard to save," it read. "America and the Earth need a hero right now, someone who will transcend politics as usual and bring real hope to our country and to the world."[59]

Despite efforts to draft him as a candidate, Gore insisted that he had no intention of returning to politics. Although he did not reject the idea of ever running for president again, he made it clear that he was happy to continue his work as an environmentalist. "I'm under no illusions that there is any position in the world with as much influence as that of president of the United States," he stated. "But I ran for president twice, and I was in politics for a quarter century, and I honestly believe that the highest and best use of my skills and experience is to try to change the minds of people in the U.S. and elsewhere in the world about this planetary emergency that we simply have to confront."[60]

A man waiting to attend an appearance by Gore in Beverly Hills, California, in May 2007 holds a sign that expresses his hope that the former presidential candidate would make a run at the White House in 2008.

Some observers suggested that Gore was reluctant to return to politics because he did not want to lose touch with the new man he had become. They noted that since he no longer felt the constraints of campaigning for office, Gore had abandoned the stiff and cautious tendencies that had made it difficult for him to connect with voters and express his true self. In his career as an environmental activist, by contrast, he is widely regarded as a passionate, fearless, visionary leader. "I came through all of that [election controversy] and I guess I changed," Gore acknowledged. "And now it is easier for me to just let it fly."[61]

Chapter 1: Two Separate Childhoods

1. Quoted in Melinda Henneberger, "Al Gore's Journey: A Boyhood Divided," *New York Times on the Web*, May 22, 2000. http://partners.nytimes.com/library/politics/camp/052200wh-dem-gore.html?scp=1&sq=Al%20GOre's%20Jo urney:%20A%20BOy's%20LIfe%20in%20and%20OUt%20 of%20the%20Family%20Script&st=cse.

2. Quoted in Henneberger, "Al Gore's Journey: A Boyhood Divided."

3. Quoted in "Albert Gore Jr.: Son of a Senator," *CNN Special Reports—Becoming Al Gore,* October 22, 2000. http://www .cnn.com/SPECIALS/2000/democracy/gore/stories/gore.

4. Quoted in Bob Zelnick, *Gore: A Political Life.* Washington, DC: Regnery Publishing, 1999, p. 29.

5. Quoted in Henneberger, "Al Gore's Journey: A Boyhood Divided."

6. Quoted in Henneberger, "Al Gore's Journey: A Boyhood Divided."

7. Quoted in "Albert Gore Jr.: Son of a Senator."

Chapter 2: From Harvard to Vietnam

8. Quoted in Melinda Henneberger, "The 2000 Campaign: A Test of Character; On Campus Torn by 60's, Agonizing Over the Path," *New York Times on the Web*, June 21, 2000. http:// query.nytimes.com/gst/fullpage.html?res=9806E4D91031F9 32A15755C0A9669C8B63&sec=&spon=&pagewanted=6.

9. Al Gore, *Earth in the Balance: Ecology and the Human Spirit.* Boston: Houghton Mifflin, 1992, p. 6.

10. Quoted in "Albert Gore Jr.: Son of a Senator."

11. Quoted in Hampton Sides, "Born to Run: The Life and Times of a Thoroughbred Politician," *Memphis*, May 1986, p. 47.

12. Quoted in Henneberger, "The 2000 Campaign."

13. Quoted in Myra MacPherson, "Al Gore and the Window of Certainty," *Washington Post*, February 3, 1988.
14. Quoted in "Albert Gore Jr.: Son of a Senator."
15. Quoted in Melinda Henneberger, "Al Gore's Journey: Off to War," *New York Times on the Web*, July 11, 2000. http://partners.nytimes.com/library/politics/camp/071100wh-gore.html.
16. Quoted in MacPherson, "Al Gore and the Window of Certainty."
17. Quoted in Sherrye Henry, "Talking to … Albert Gore, Jr.," *Vogue*, May 1988, p. 62.

Chapter 3: Following in His Father's Footsteps

18. Quoted in Alex S. Jones, "Al Gore's Double Life," *New York Times Magazine*, October 25, 1992, p. 79.
19. Quoted in Frank Sutherland, "Albert Gore Jr. Starts Drive for Evins's Seat," *Nashville Tennessean*, March 2, 1976.
20. Quoted in Bill Turque, *Inventing Al Gore*. Boston: Houghton Mifflin, 2000, p. 125.
21. Quoted in "The Son Makes His Mark," *CNN Special Reports—Becoming Al Gore*, October 22, 2000. http://www.cnn.com/SPECIALS/2000/democracy/gore/stories/gore/index1.html.
22. Quoted in "The Son Makes His Mark."
23. Al Gore, "1992 Vice Presidential Acceptance Speech." http://www.al-gore-2004.org/gorespeeches/1992convention.htm.
24. Quoted in Richard L. Berke, "The Good Son," *New York Times Magazine*, February 20, 1994, p. 44.
25. Gore, *Earth in the Balance*, p. 8.
26. Gore, *Earth in the Balance*, p. 9.
27. Quoted in "The First Presidential Run," *CNN Special Reports—Becoming Al Gore*, October 22, 2000. http://www.cnn.com/SPECIALS/2000/democracy/gore/stories/gore/index2.html.
28. Quoted in Jones, "Al Gore's Double Life," p. SM40.
29. Al Gore, "Facing the Crisis of Spirit," *Vital Speeches of the Day*, August 15, 1992, p. 648.
30. Gore, *Earth in the Balance*, p. 12.

Chapter 4: The Clinton-Gore Years

31. Quoted in David Maraniss and Ellen Nakashima, *The Prince of Tennessee: The Rise of Al Gore*. New York: Simon and Schuster, 2000, p. 270.
32. Quoted in Zelnick, *Gore: A Political Life*, p. 216.
33. Gore, "Facing the Crisis of Spirit," p. 648.
34. Quoted in S.C. Gwynne and Elizabeth Taylor, "We're Not Measuring the Drapes," *Time*, October 19, 1992, p. 36.
35. Quoted in Walter Shapiro, "Has Anyone Seen This Man?" *Esquire*, September 1993, p. 116.
36. Quoted in "Clinton's Number Two," *CNN Special Reports— Becoming Al Gore*, October 22, 2000. http://www.cnn.com/SPECIALS/2000/democracy/gore/stories/gore/index3.html.
37. Quoted in Shapiro, "Has Anyone Seen This Man?" p. 116.
38. Quoted in Turque, *Inventing Al Gore*, p. 336.
39. Bill Clinton, speech delivered August 17, 1998. http://www.cnn.com/ALLPOLITICS/1998/08/17/speech/transcript.html.
40. Quoted in "Clinton's Number Two."
41. Quoted in Andy Walton, "Two Years in the Life of Al Jr.," *CNN Special Reports—Becoming Al Gore*, October 22, 2000. http://www.cnn.com/SPECIALS/2000/democracy/gore/stories/gore.odyssey/.

Chapter 5: The 2000 Election

42. Quoted in Kenneth T. Walsh, "Is He Clinton's Real Legacy?" *U.S. News and World Report*, September 8, 1997, p. 22.
43. Quoted in James W. Ceaser and Andrew E. Busch, *The Perfect Tie: The True Story of the 2000 Presidential Election*. Lanham, MD: Rowman and Littlefield, 2001, p. 31.
44. Quoted in Eric Alterman, *What Liberal Media? The Truth About Bias and the News*. New York: Basic Books, 2003, p. 171.
45. Quoted in Ceaser and Busch, *The Perfect Tie*, p. 198.
46. Quoted in Ceaser and Busch, *The Perfect Tie*, p. 199.
47. Quoted in Phil Hirschkorn, "Crowds Line Up for Clinton Book," *CNN.com*, June 22, 2004. http://www.cnn.com/2004/ALLPOLITICS/06/22/clinton.book/index.html.

48. Lee Edwards, "The Closest Presidential Election Ever," *World and I*, February 2001, p. 20.

Chapter 6: Champion of the Environment

49. Quoted in Karen Breslau, "The Resurrection of Al Gore," *Wired*, May 2006. http://www.wired.com/wired/archive/14.05/gore. html.
50. Quoted in Breslau, "The Resurrection of Al Gore."
51. Al Gore, *The Assault on Reason*. New York: Penguin, 2007, p. 2.
52. Quoted in Karen Tumulty, "Al Gore: Businessman," *Time*, August 6, 2005, p. 32.
53. Eric Pooley, "The Last Temptation of Al Gore," *Time*, May 28, 2007, p. 30.
54. Quoted in Pooley, "The Last Temptation of Al Gore," p. 31.
55. Quoted in "Gore Uses Oscar Speech to Plug Environmental Cause," *CNN.com*, February 26, 2007. http://www.cnn .com/2007/POLITICS/02/26/gore.oscar/index.html.
56. Quoted in Walter Gibbs and Sarah Lyall, "Gore Shares Peace Prize for Climate Work," *New York Times*, October 13, 2007. http://www.nytimes.com/2007/10/13/world/13nobel.html/.
57. Quoted in Gibbs and Lyall, "Gore Shares Peace Prize for Climate Work."
58. Quoted in Bryan Walsh, "The Gore Interview," *Time*, December 21, 2007, p. 98.
59. Quoted in "Gore: Nobel Win a Chance 'to Change the Way People Think,'" *CNN.com*, October 12, 2007. http://www.cnn. com/2007/POLITICS/10/12/nobel.gore/index.html.
60. Quoted in Ed O'Keefe, "Environmental Al Gore Is Back," *abcnews.com*, June 4, 2006. http://abcnews.go.com/ThisWeek/ Politics/story?id=2037158.
61. Quoted in Pooley, "The Last Temptation of Al Gore," p. 31.

1948

Albert Alfred Gore Jr. is born on March 31 in Washington, D.C.

1965

Gore graduates from an exclusive Washington prep school, St. Albans Episcopal School for Boys, and enters Harvard University.

1968

Gore first learns about global warming in a college science course taught by Professor Roger Revelle.

1969

After graduating from Harvard with a bachelor's degree in government, Gore enlists in the U.S. Army on August 7.

1970

Gore marries Mary Elizabeth Aitcheson, known as Tipper, on May 19.

1971

On January 2, Gore arrives in Vietnam for a tour of duty as an army journalist. Five months later, he receives an honorable discharge and returns to the United States.

1976

After working as a newspaper reporter and taking classes toward a law degree, Gore decides to launch a career in politics. Tennessee voters elect him to serve in the U.S. House of Representatives. He remains in office for four terms.

1984

Gore campaigns successfully to represent Tennessee in the U.S. Senate. He is reelected in 1990.

1988

Gore runs for president of the United States but fails to win the Democratic Party nomination.

1989

Gore's youngest child, Albert, is hit by a car and suffers severe injuries. During his son's recovery, Gore writes a book, *Earth in the Balance*, outlining his environmental views.

1992

Democratic presidential nominee Bill Clinton chooses Gore as his vice presidential running mate. The Clinton-Gore ticket marches to victory in the general election.

2000

After serving two terms as an active and influential vice president under Clinton, Gore receives the Democratic presidential nomination. In one of the closest and most controversial elections in U.S. history, Gore wins the popular vote but loses the presidency to Republican candidate George W. Bush.

2006

Gore appears in the documentary film *An Inconvenient Truth*, which chronicles his efforts to raise public awareness of the threat of global climate change. The film wins several awards, including the 2007 Academy Award for Best Documentary Feature.

2007

Gore receives the prestigious Nobel Peace Prize for his crusade to prevent global warming, making him the world's best-known environmental activist.

Books

Al Gore, *The Assault on Reason*. New York: Penguin, 2007. In this critique of American democracy, Gore argues that the modern political system has moved dangerously far away from what the nation's founders intended.

Al Gore, *Earth in the Balance: Ecology and the Human Spirit*. Boston: Houghton Mifflin, 1992. In his first published book, Gore outlines the environmental views that eventually shaped his life outside of politics.

David Maraniss and Ellen Nakashima, *The Prince of Tennessee: The Rise of Al Gore*. New York: Simon and Schuster, 2000. This biography examines Gore's early life and the ways in which it prepared him for a career in politics.

Kate McMullan, *The Story of Bill Clinton and Al Gore: Our Nation's Leaders*. Milwaukee: Gareth Stevens, 1996. Intended for students, this readable biography follows the lives of the president and vice president through the conclusion of their first term in office.

Periodicals

Karen Breslau, "The Resurrection of Al Gore," *Wired*, May 2006. This lengthy feature follows Gore's efforts to transform himself and his career in the wake of the 2000 election.

Eric Pooley, "The Last Temptation of Al Gore," *Time*, May 28, 2007, p. 30. This *Time* magazine cover story details Gore's life after the 2000 election, from his high-profile environmental campaign to Democratic Party efforts to draft him as a presidential candidate in 2008.

Web Sites

Al Gore (http://www.algore.com). Gore's official site includes a brief biography, a journal, and information about his various books, projects, and business interests.

"Al Gore's Journey," New York Times on the Web (http://

partners.nytimes.com/library/politics/camp/052200wh-
dem-gore.html?scp=1&sq=Al%20GOre's%20Journey:%20A%
20BOy's%20LIfe%20in%20and%20OUt%20of%20the%20Fa
mily%20Script&st=cse). This site includes a series of in-depth
articles about Gore's childhood, college years, military service,
and career in politics.

**"Becoming Al Gore," CNN Special Reports—Democracy in
America** (http://www.cnn.com/SPECIALS/2000/democracy/
gore/stories/gore). This extensive series of biographical features
appeared a few weeks prior to the 2000 election. It includes
Gore's family tree, a timeline of events in Gore's life, information about Gore's political record, and lengthy articles covering
key periods of Gore's life.

An Inconvenient Truth (http://www.climatecrisis.net/
aboutthefilm). The official site of the award-winning
documentary film features scientific background about global
warming, a companion educational guide, and information
about ways to help combat the climate crisis.

About the Author

Laurie Collier Hillstrom is a partner in Northern Lights Writers Group, a freelance writing and editorial services firm based in Brighton, Michigan. She has written and edited award-winning reference works on a wide range of subjects, including American history, biography, popular culture, and international environmental issues. Recent works include *Frida Kahlo: Mexican Portrait Artist* (Lucent/Gale, 2007); *The Thanksgiving Book* (Omnigraphics, 2007); *Television in American Society Reference Library* (3 volumes, UXL/Gale, 2006), and *The Industrial Revolution in America* (9 volumes, ABC-Clio, 2005-07).